Presented To:

_____

_____

From:

_____

_____

Date:

_____

Tea Time with God

Tulsa, Oklahoma

2nd Printing
Over 165,000 in Print

Tea Time with God

ISBN 1-56292-033-2

Copyright © 1996 by Honor Books, Inc.

P.O. Box 55388

Tulsa, Ok 74155

Manuscript prepared by W. B. Freeman Concepts, Inc., Tulsa, Oklahoma.

Cover Illustration by Taylor Bruce

"Tea for Two"

Thinking of "tea time" evokes pleasant memories of friendships steeping over a hot pot of tea. With the image of a beautifully laid table set with Grandmother's fine china and silver, we recall a finer time of civility, gentility, propriety — when life made perfect sense.

While not everyone observes a formal afternoon tea time, the tradition of breaking for a small repast of tea and cakes can benefit anyone. The rush of the day's activity slows for a moment, shared conversation with a friend turns our thoughts toward being instead of doing, and peace is reestablished in our lives. It is a time to repair our frayed nerves and restore order to a fractured day.

Spending a few moments in the afternoon with the Lord can begin with reviewing the day's events so far. Get any negatives out of the way first, such as a hasty affront to a coworker or a missed opportunity for doing good. Pray for forgiveness and the opportunity to make restitution. Then express gratitude to God for the prayers he has answered and for His help.

Any time, any day, is a good time for praise, thanksgiving, and forgiveness — but especially so when the heat of the day still lingers and our souls are weary. Let this book be your *Tea Time With God* — to refresh yourself in the Lord before you enter the final hours of your day.

Tea for at Least Two

He leadeth me beside the still waters.
He restoreth my soul.
Psalm 23:2-3

The brief respite known as afternoon tea is said to have been the creation of Anna, Duchess of Bedford, in the nineteenth century. At that time the English customarily ate a hearty breakfast, paused for a light lunch at midday, and didn't return to the table until late evening. Understandably hungry long before dinner, the duchess asked to have a small meal served in her private quarters in the late afternoon. Eventually, she invited close friends to share the repast. The sensible custom was quickly adopted throughout England.

While the Duchess' initiation of tea time was aimed at nourishment of her body, she and the rest of England soon discovered that adding beautiful china and good friends to the occasion also nourished the soul. In fact, the real value of formal tea time lies in its ability to enrich and brighten the everyday routine by stressing the importance of courtesy and friendship.[1]

We are wise to recognize our need for a "spiritual tea time" each day. Even if we have a "hearty breakfast" in the Word each morning, there may be times when the pressures of the day come to bear in late afternoon. Our spirits long for a little peace and refreshment in the presence of our loving Savior. Just as enjoying a muffin with a few sips of tea can give something of a lift to our lagging physical energy level, a quick prayer or the voicing of praise can give our spirit a lift.

Set aside some time in the middle of the afternoon to turn your attention to the beauty of life that the Lord has set before you. Find beauty and comfort in the people around you, the flowers on a table, or simply the delicious aroma of tea brewing. Create a few moments away from the hustle and bustle of your life before returning to the tasks that await you. Give thanks to the Lord for sharing His presence with you.

Finishing Strong

And when Jesus had cried with a loud voice, he said,
"Father, into thy hands I commend my spirit:"
and having said thus, he gave up the ghost.
Luke 23:46

The Gospel accounts of Matthew, Mark, and Luke tell us that Jesus ended His earthly life and ministry by crying with a loud voice, obviously from a great surge of energy. Luke tells us further that in His cry, Jesus commended His spirit to the Lord, giving His all to the Father.

What a wonderful example of how we might end our work each day!

First, we need to "finish strong." In the afternoon, we often must refocus and double our efforts. Those who work in offices often find their most productive hour is the last hour of the day when everyone else has gone home and the phone has stopped ringing. Those who work at home also tend to experience an end-of-the-day urgency to get things done before shifting to more relaxed hours.

We are wise to pray as we enter the home stretch of a day, "Father, give me Your strength and energy to bring to a conclusion what I have started. Help me now to go the extra mile."

Second, we need to commend our work to the Lord. As we finish our work, we need to say, "Thank You, Lord, for the energy, health, and creativity to do what I have done today. Now, I turn over all rights to what I have done to You. I trust You to winnow out what is worthless, and to cause that which is worthy to last and benefit others. I give it all to You."

To finish strong and commend our work to the Lord requires humility. We must recognize that the Lord is the source of all our ability and power to accomplish and succeed.

As you pause this afternoon, choose to finish your day well, and then give what you have done to the Lord.

Power Steering

*For whatever is born of God overcomes the world; and this is
the victory that has overcome the world — our faith.*
1 John 5:4 (NASB)

Few things in life make us feel as powerful as
sitting behind the steering wheel of a car. Realizing the
vehicle weighs two tons and is capable of traveling up
to 100 miles per hour, we have a tendency to feel
almost invincible — which is a good feeling after a
long, hard day at work.

Unfortunately, this heady sensation often results in
dangerous or rude behavior, such as changing lanes
without signaling, driving too fast, tailgating, failing to
yield to merging traffic, running red lights or stop
signs, flashing headlights, and blaring horns. When we
give in to the urge to do just one of these things,
reasoning, "It won't hurt to do it this once," or "I'm in
a hurry," or "Everyone else does it," we become part of
a problem instead of part of a solution.

Power Steering

How should you act when you're in the driver's seat at the end of your work day, headed for home? Pop some uplifting music (such as praise songs) into the tape deck, or listen to the soothing sounds of a classical station. Say a quick prayer before you start the engine ("Father, give me a safe journey home") and decide you'll be a friendly, courteous driver and not a road hazard. Use this time for personal rejoicing over the work you've just completed.

What do you do when other drivers seem to be going out of their way to make your drive time a "drive-you-crazy" time? Resist the urge to scream, shake your fist, or respond in kind to whatever the offending driver does. Say a prayer for him, smile, and wave. Let him wonder if he knows you from somewhere!

Have faith in God to turn any problem into a blessing. You'll have a much nicer evening when you finally arrive home!

Take Time for Beauty

One thing I have desired of the Lord, that will I seek:...
to behold the beauty of the Lord.
Psalm 27:4 (NKJV)

"Keep a place in life for beauty," says English preacher Leslie Weatherhead. "He who keeps a little place in his life for beauty will find that it does something for him and in him, and that something is a process that goes on when the beauty is no longer before his eyes and ears, like a seed growing secretly in the dark. God, by a secret ministry, can turn the sight of a snowflake into hope and the sight of the dawn into courage."[2]

Beauty feeds our souls like food nourishes our bodies. Beauty points us to the transcendent, takes us beyond our finiteness and opens our hearts to that which is greater and larger than ourselves. There is something about great beauty that brings into the awesome presence of the infinite and the eternal.

In reflecting on his priorities, a prominent British scientist said he would give more time to the enjoyment of things that are beautiful: "If I had my life to live over again, I would have made a rule to read some poetry and listen to some music at least once a week; for perhaps the part of my brain now atrophied would have thus been kept active through use. The loss of these tastes is a loss of happiness, and may possibly be injurious to the intellect, and more probably to the moral character, by enfeebling the emotional part of our nature."[3]

We sometimes need to be reminded to slow down enough to find beauty in those things we hurry by each day. Let's take time for beauty. Make a date with yourself to stroll through an art gallery, visit a beautiful church, or linger in a park or garden.

If there simply is not time, then remember the beautiful places captured in memories — moments of sheer joy, or a mental "snapshot" of a majestic, snow-capped mountain or moonlit night.

Let God use the beauty He created to awaken in you the desire for more of Him.

Listen for the Music

*How shall we sing the Lord's song
in a strange land?*

Psalm 137:4

George Gershwin was talking to a friend on the crowded beach of a resort near New York City when the joyous shrieks of voices pierced their conversation. Clanking tunes ground out from a nearby merry-go-round while barkers and hucksters shouted themselves hoarse. From underground came the deep roar of the subway; beside them crashed the relentless waves of the ocean.

Gershwin listened and then remarked to his friend, "All of this could form such a beautiful pattern of sound. It could turn into a magnificent musical piece expressive of every human activity and feeling with pauses, counterpoints, blends and climaxes of sound that would be beautiful...But it is not that...It is all discordant, terrible and exhausting — as we hear it now. The pattern is always being shattered."

What a parable of our time! So many confusing sounds and noises, so much unrest, so much rapid change. But somewhere in the midst of it, a pattern could emerge; a meaning could come out of it.

Our job is to hear the music in the noise.

Sometimes, finding the melodic line is a simple matter of listening selectively — mentally tuning out all but one sound for awhile. That's what happens when we sit for a few minutes over a cup of tea and listen intently to that coworker, employee, or child. Once we listen and truly hear the "tune" they're playing, their unique melody will always be distinct to us, even in the cacophony of busy days.

If we are intentional about what we hear, the conflicting chaos swirling around our own symphony will be weeded out; God's music will be easier to hear.

In the midst of a busy day, it takes effort to hear all the melodies of those around you which make up the symphony of your life. But as each strain becomes distinguishable, a pattern emerges, and you can rejoice in God's unparalleled creativity in His world.

This afternoon, sip your tea and be a creative listener!

Good for What Ails You

*My command is this: Love each other
as I have loved you.*
John 15:12 (NIV)

For God so loved the world... (John 3:16). Do you wonder sometimes how He can love all of us? Have you ever met anyone who seemed determined to be as unlovable as possible?

A woman who dearly loved her husband and son was having a very hard time loving her mother-in-law. The mother-in-law had decided that no woman was good enough for her son. She took every opportunity to remind the daughter-in-law of her opinion.

One day, the mother-in-law got the flu. She did not require hospitalization, but she was bedridden. Because her husband's work hours prevented him from caring for her, he decided to bring her to his house so his wife could take on the responsibility.

Mom had the audacity to bring her own food, subtly implying she did not trust her daughter-in-law's cooking. Undaunted, the daughter-in-law set aside the store-bought food and got to work, preparing a mouth-watering pot of homemade chicken soup and a loaf of homemade bread. She served these delicacies in her best china, with the company-only, gleaming silverware, on a lace-covered tray.

Needless to say, Mom was shocked to be the recipient of such an elegantly presented meal. After several days of this service, her feelings toward her daughter-in-law softened. Although it was the dead of winter, the spring thaw came early that year![4]

If you have someone who has been a challenge for you to love today, think of something extraordinarily nice you could do for them. Pray for them, and determine in your heart that no matter what happens, you will love them as unconditionally as God loves you.

No Longer Enemies

The wolf also shall dwell with the lamb, and the leopard shall lie down with the kid; and the calf and the young lion and the fatling together; and a little child shall lead them.

Isaiah 11:6

The orange kitten was hungry. The grizzly bear was lonely. The man was apprehensive.

The cat weighed no more than 10 ounces when he first slid under the fence into the bear's pen. The man was almost in a panic thinking the hungry grizzly would kill him with one swat and eat him for dinner — carnivorous bears make much larger animals a part of their diet.

The grizzly, whose name was Griz, had come to the Oregon wildlife center in 1990 when he was just a cub. Hit by a train while foraging on railroad tracks in Montana, he suffered severe head injuries and was deemed unfit to return to the wild.

The kitten was one of four kittens abandoned at the center early in the summer. Volunteers were able to find homes for the rest of the litter, but Cat, as he was now called, somehow eluded them.

Then one day in July, Cat turned up in Griz's pen. Afraid to do anything that might alarm Griz, the man just watched, expecting the worst. As the 650-pound grizzly was eating his midday meal, something extraordinary happened. The bear very gently picked out a chicken wing with his forepaw and dropped it near Cat.

From that moment on, Griz and Cat became something of a slapstick animal act. Cat would lay in ambush, then leap out and swat Griz on his nose. Griz would carry Cat in his mouth. Cat would ride on Griz's back, and sometimes Griz would lick Cat.

Their friendly relationship defies both the patterns of nature as well as their own troubled life histories. Griz never took advantage of Cat's weaknesses, and each animal has accommodated the other's needs.[5]

What a lesson Griz and Cat offer! We can help each other break free from the patterns of our past that keep us from loving each other. As we pray for and care for others with the love of Jesus Christ, we obtain healing by the grace of God, both for them and ourselves!

Pass It On!

Then our mouth was filled with laughter,
and our tongue with shouts of joy.
Psalm 126:2 (RSV)

On the first day of his cruise in the Caribbean, a man entering his senior years noticed an attractive woman about his age. She gave him a friendly smile as he passed her on the deck.

That evening at dinner, he was seated at the same table with her. To make conversation, he commented that he had appreciated her kind smile during his afternoon walk. When she heard this, she said, "The reason I smiled was that when I saw you, I was immediately struck by your strong resemblance to my third husband."

"Oh," he said. "How many times have you been married?" he asked with interest.

She looked down at her dinner plate, a slight smile crossed her face, and she tentatively answered, "Twice."

A smile is a great encourager!

An unknown author said it well:

"*A smile costs nothing, but gives much. It enriches those who receive, without making poorer those who give. It takes but a moment, but the memory of it sometimes lasts forever. None is so rich or mighty that they can get along without it, and none is so poor but that they can be made rich by it.*

"*A smile creates happiness in the home, fosters good will in business, and is the countersign of friendship. It brings rest to the weary, cheer to the discouraged, sunshine to the sad, and it is nature's antidote for trouble. Yet it cannot be bought, begged, borrowed, or stolen, for it is something that is of no value to anyone until it is given away. Some people are too tired to give you a smile. Give them one of yours, as none needs a smile so much as the one who has no more to give.*"

Have you been grumpy today? Ask God for a double dose of His joy and then put a smile on your face. Let people know you refuse to take on the negativism or cynicism of the world. You can be cheerful and pass that cheer on to others with a simple smile.

The Evening Sacrifice

Let my prayer be set before You as incense,
the lifting up of my hands as the evening sacrifice.
Psalm 141:2 (NKJV)

The time of the evening sacrifice at the Temple in Jerusalem was from 3:00 to 6:00 p.m. It was during this time period that the unblemished lambs were sacrificed each spring during Passover. The sacrifice was required to be complete before sunset, which was considered the start of a new day.

It was also during this time that Jesus gave His life on the cross outside Jerusalem. The Gospel writers tell us He died after the "ninth hour" (3:00 in the afternoon) and His body was removed from the cross before the official close of the day.

On the cross, Jesus was the unblemished "lamb slain from the foundation of the world" (Revelation 13:8 NKJV). Christian believers worldwide recognize Him as the perfect sacrifice for their sins, but Jesus also initiated a "new day" between God and man. Man would no longer be separated from God because of sin and guilt, and God could once again have fellowship with those who believed on His Son.

The evening sacrifice marked the end of separation and a new beginning. As you leave your place of work today or move from one set of chores to another, make it a point to say "good-bye" in a tangible way to the day that is past. That may mean closing the office door, turning off the light, or just switching off your pager.

Embrace the new day by leaving the previous day behind. Whatever you have accomplished today is your "sacrifice" of time, energy, ability, and resources to your Lord and Savior. Mark its end with a firm "Amen."

That Loving Touch

He hath said, I will never leave thee, nor forsake thee.
Hebrews 13:5

*B*eing a flawed human being isn't easy. Around tea time, when our energy is a bit low, we are more likely to recognize all ways we've failed during the day. Sometimes we wonder how our heavenly Father puts up with all of our inadequacies.

A minister told of a certain family in his church who had waited a long time for a child. The couple was overjoyed when at last a son was born to them, but they were crushed when they learned he had a severe handicap. He would go into extremely violent seizures without warning. Nevertheless, as he grew they tried to make his life as normal as possible.

Whenever the church doors were open, this family could be found in attendance. As time passed, the child developed a deep love for the same Jesus his parents loved, and he counted on Him to bring him through each of his life-threatening episodes.

The minister tells of the father's love as reflected on one particular Sunday:

"I remember the father always holding the little boy during worship at our church. I remember one particularly hard seizure when the father gently but firmly held the little guy and went to the back of the sanctuary. There he held him to his chest, gently whispering into his ear. There was no hint of embarrassment or frustration on that father's face. Only calm, deep, abiding love."

That is a picture of our heavenly Father's love for us. In spite of our deep imperfections, He is not embarrassed to call us His children. He tenderly holds us through the deepest, hardest part of our struggles and whispers words of assurance and encouragement while He clutches us to Himself and supports us with His loving care.

Unearthing Resources

Blessed are those who hunger and thirst for righteousness,
for they shall be satisfied.
Matthew 5:6 (RSV)

*M*embers of a mountaineering club were planning to build a cabin in the mountains. One hot August afternoon they went out to the building site to look for a water source for the proposed structure. There had been a small spring at the foot of the hill where the cabin was to be built, but on that dry summer day all they found was a steady little trickle.

One of the club members thought the trickle was just drainage off the hillside and doubted if there really was an underground spring. Another climber noticed there was not just one trickle but several, which wasn't much proof of an underground stream. Still a third member thought they might find the stream, but questioned whether it was large enough for a dependable water supply.

As unpromising as the prospect seemed, they found no other possible water source, so they agreed to begin digging. Shovelsful of topsoil were removed down to the sandy soil where the trickles got much larger. When they followed each one to its source they found that all the trickles converged into a single underground pool fed by a spring.

The crew worked hard and quickly that afternoon, walling up the underground spring with stone and concrete to make a wellhole. In less than an hour the well filled to capacity, holding fifty gallons. It would provide a reliable supply of cool, refreshing water.

People of all ages have looked in many places to find a fountain of life from which to draw the resources and strength required for living. Jesus said, "If any one thirst, let him come to me and drink. He who believes in me, as the scripture has said, 'Out of his heart shall flow rivers of living water'" (John 7:37-38 RSV).

Stand Up!

Mark the perfect man, and behold the upright:
for the end of that man is peace.
Psalm 37:37

People who primarily spend their day sitting can find themselves to be mind-and-body weary around 4:00 p.m., just as much as those who have spent most of the day walking or moving about. As a result, most sitters find that a short walk or a short time of standing provides them with the refreshment they need to finish the day well.

Do you know that standing does more than keep muscles from cramping?

The next time you need to make a quick or complex decision, stand up! That's the advice of Max Vercruyssen, a work performance expert at the University of Southern California in Los Angeles. The reason? Regular "stand up and stretch" breaks, or even working while standing up, can improve work performance.

Stand Up!

Vercruyssen studied sixty people faced with tasks that demanded information processing and decisions. He found that by standing up:

- they absorbed information 40 percent quicker,

- they improved their perceptions, and

- those over the age of 60 gained an edge in performing simple tasks.

Any number of physiological reasons can explain why performance is enhanced by standing up — such as the fact that there are fewer interruptions in blood flowing to and from the brain. The lungs expand more fully when we stand and the very act of standing up causes us to take deeper breaths.

Standing has an important spiritual and emotional effect as well. Jesus often told people He had healed to get up — stand! Standing up can trigger an inner surge of confidence in ourselves and in the Holy Spirit who works within us. It also can signify acceptance of responsibility for the tasks the Lord has put before us. Standing signals readiness and conviction.

When you need a brain and body booster — don't just sit there — stand up!

Sugar or Lemon?

These six things doth the Lord hate: yea,
seven are an abomination unto him: A proud look,
a lying tongue, and hands that shed innocent blood,
an heart that deviseth wicked imaginations, feet that be
swift in running to mischief, a false witness that speaketh
lies, and he that soweth discord among brethren.
Proverbs 6:16-19

Afternoon tea is traditionally a time for reflecting on the day and chatting with friends. Perhaps because it comes at a low-energy time of day, we may be more careless in our conversation and include not-so-kind opinions about others.

At the very time sugar and cream are being slipped into the tea, verbal raspberries, lemons, and sour grapes may slip into the conversation.

Consider sharing this little poem with your tea-mates at the beginning of your time together.

I Know Something Good About You

Wouldn't this world be better,
If folks whom we meet would say
"I know something good about you,"
And treat you just that way?

Wouldn't it be splendid,
If each handshake, good and true,
Carried with it this assurance:
"I know something good about you?"

Wouldn't life be happier,
If the good that's in us all,
Were the only thing about us
That people would recall?

Wouldn't our days be sweeter,
If we praised the good we see;
For there is a lot of goodness,
In the worst of you and me?

Wouldn't it be fine to practice,
This way of thinking too;
You know something good about me,
I know something good about you?

Unknown

Sticks and Stones

*Yet in all these things we are more than
conquerors through Him who loved us.*
Romans 8:37 (NKJV)

Have you noticed how a project can seem to
expand? You break a job down into small parts and get
most of those done, but during the day other elements
are added to the mix. Before you know it, a
straightforward task is out of control.

It's a lot like clearing a field before building a house.
There are trees to chop down, roots to dig up, and
rocks to clear away. After several weeks of digging and
lifting and raking, it appears the work is done and the
land is ready. Then a major rainstorm washes away
some layers of dirt, or a cold snap pushes more rocks to
the surface. Your cleared field is suddenly dotted with
rocks, stones, and sticks. And so it goes, often for years.

How do you cope with a field that won't stay
cleared, or a job that never seems to end? The fact is,

most jobs do have a beginning, a middle, and an end. It helps to remember that![6]

Don't allow the interruptions and additions to paralyze your progress. The field is eventually clear enough to build the house, the report is put together, the test is completed, the results are analyzed, the product is manufactured.

The apostle Paul knew a little bit about overcoming obstacles that threatened to make his job impossible. In 2 Corinthians 11:23-29, he outlines some of the hardships he endured in his mission to spread the Gospel: imprisonment, floggings, exposure to death, lashings, stoning, shipwrecks, lack of sleep, hunger, and thirst. Most believers would quit if a couple of these things happened to them, but not Paul.

Paul wrote that "we are God's workmanship" — a work in progress! — "created in Christ Jesus to do good works, which God prepared in advance for us to do" (Ephesians 2:10 NIV).

When we face a job with multiple components and no clear end in sight, we do well to recall God can give us the strength to handle our own works in progress. The One who made us will give us all we need to complete every job.

End-of-Work Prayer

In all your ways acknowledge Him.
Proverbs 3:6 (NKJV)

Many people are quick to pray before a meal, before they begin a new project, before they attempt something for the first time, or before embarking on a long journey. They desire to start on the right foot, asking for God's help, protection, creativity, and blessing, but what about prayer at the end of a work day, journey, or task?

Such a prayer is like a second bookend on a shelf of freestanding books — it brackets our work and brings us to full recognition that we have received from the Lord the very things we requested. Rather than be a prayer of petition, such a prayer is an expression of praise and thanksgiving.

Simeon had lived his entire life waiting to see the Messiah — a promise the Lord had made to him. (See Luke 2:26.) Upon seeing the infant Jesus in the

Temple, Simeon took Him in his arms, blessed God, and said, "Lord, now You are letting Your servant depart in peace, according to Your word; for my eyes have seen Your salvation" (Luke 2:29-30 NKJV). Simeon recognized that God had been faithful to His Word, and his heart was encouraged and filled with joy.

Simeon is a wonderful example of how we need to begin and end the events of our lives with prayer. When we reach the end of a day, haggard and weary, we can remember Simeon's prayer, "Lord, let Your servant depart in peace, according to Your Word."

Knowing God was with us today and He will be with us tomorrow, we can move on to the evening hours with freedom and a sense of satisfaction.

Vantage Point

> *Iron sharpeneth iron; so a man sharpeneth*
> *the countenance of his friend.*
> *Proverbs 27:17*

*M*iss Mildred, an eighty-five-year-old resident of Nova Scotia, is a constant reminder to former Undersecretary of the Interior John C. Whitaker that he should not take himself too seriously. She has lived her life in one location, where the population swells to nine in the summer and stays steady at two in the winter.

Whitaker, who has been fishing in Nova Scotia every year since he was twelve, flew in one day for a few hours of recreation. Miss Mildred welcomed him into her kitchen and said, "Johnny, I hate to admit I don't know, but where is Washington?"

When Whitaker realized she wasn't kidding, he explained: "That's where the President of the United States lives — just as the Prime Minister of Canada lives in Ottawa."

When she asked how many people lived there, Whitaker said there were about two million residents. She responded, "Think of that...two million people living so far away from everything."[7]

Our perspective on the world and the actions of others is always seen through our frame of reference, which is shaped by our life experiences. When we must live or work with someone who has a completely different viewpoint, it is easy to be critical.

This is the time when we need to ask God to give us His point of view. Through His eyes, we can see people who are very different from us with more understanding and compassion. The most difficult, frustrating relationships in our lives can be put into a calm and reasonable perspective.

When we ask God to open our eyes to the other person's outlook on life, an interesting thing happens to us. Our own life experience becomes richer and our capacity to relate to others enlarges.

To Your Health

If you have anything against anyone, forgive him.
Mark 11:25 (NKJV)

According to a popular children's song, tea is a "drink with jam and bread." But in a recently released study, nutritionists recommend you have an apple rather than jam and bread with your tea. The Dutch research group found that drinking tea and eating apples together reduces the risk of stroke.

The newly completed study showed health benefits resulted from long-term consumption of black tea — the type most Americans and Europeans drink. Drinking tea, plus eating other fruits and vegetables containing flavonoids, lowered the incidence of strokes. Flavonoids make blood cell platelets less likely to clot and act as antioxidants, which reduce damage to arteries.

Four-fifths of all strokes result from blood clots, which can lodge in arteries that have been narrowed by damaging oxidation. Flavonoids found in tea and fruit inhibit blood clots and minimize damage to arteries from oxidation, thus allowing a healthy flow of blood and oxygen to the body.

Our spiritual and emotional well-being also depend on good circulation: positive thoughts which keep our minds and hearts healthy. Any blockages that would prevent a life-affirming outlook need to be dislodged.

Experts tell us that unforgiveness is one of the biggest obstacles to mental and spiritual health. Author and professor Lewis Smedes outlines four steps to forgiveness:

- Confront your anger, don't deny it.
- Separate the wrongdoer from the wrong. Be angry at the deed, not the doer.
- Let go of the past. Once we have forgiven, we can more easily forget.
- Don't give up on forgiveness — keep working at it. The deeper the hurt, the longer it takes. But keep working at it. You will realize a new attitude.

Smedes adds, "Forgiveness breaks pain's grip on our minds and opens the door to possibility...to heal the hurt and create a new beginning."[8]

A Moment of Silence

The God of peace be with you all.
Romans 15:33

The marriage is going through one of its "trying times." The kids are having trouble in school. There's too much month left at the end of the money. The roof of the house has developed an untraceable leak. The boss is making impossible demands. Wouldn't it be wonderful if you could run away from home — just for a little while?

A man named Alex was having difficulties similar to the ones listed above. His first inclination was to call his good friend, Peter. Late one afternoon, during a walk around the lake, he poured out his heart and shared his pain with the person he knew he could trust.

What did Peter say while Alex unburdened himself? Almost nothing. He knew he couldn't wave a magic wand and solve Alex's problems, and he was also wise enough to know that in some situations, saying very little is a better healing balm than empty words of sympathy. For Alex, spending a short time with a friend who simply listened was all the therapy he needed.

When Alex ran out of words, Peter's silence helped him to find a silence of his own — and some of the peace and quiet and stillness he so desperately needed. He also learned a lesson that day: how to listen to the people in his life.[9]

The American philosopher Eugene Kennedy has said: "We can master the art of being quiet in order to be able to hear clearly what others are saying....to cut off the garbled static of our own preoccupations to give to people who want our quiet attention."

Thoughtful silence can help us find solutions, or it can simply remind us that for some heartaches, there are no words to express the pain or provide a quick end to the suffering. Better than words is the love of God and His never-ending compassion...characteristics expressed through His willing-to-listen children.

Under Water

But he knoweth the way that I take: when he
hath tried me, I shall come forth as gold.
Job 23:10

*T*ea time is a wonderful time to regroup, rethink, and refresh. It comes at the time of day when we are a bit frayed from the day's activities, but the activities are not yet at an end. Unfortunately, not all of us can stop for a real tea break, but without this break, the remaining tasks may threaten to take us "under."

As the shadows of the day grow longer, our tempers can grow short. Drawing on the refreshing power of the Holy Spirit, however, will get us to the end of a stressful day. We can gain renewed patience, a fresh sense of humor, and a new surge of creativity and insight by enlisting the aid of the Spirit's ministry within us. Frequently it's during those late afternoon hours when we most need His extra help.

Jewelers claim one of the surest tests for diamonds is the underwater test. "An imitation diamond is never so brilliant as a genuine stone. If your eye is not experienced to detect the difference, a simple test is to place the stone under water. The imitation diamond is practically extinguished, while a genuine diamond sparkles even under water and is distinctly visible. If a genuine stone is placed beside an imitation one under water, the contrast will be apparent to the least experienced eye."

That is how it should be with the Christian when his head is "under water" at the end of the day. The power of the Holy Spirit can so sparkle within him, refreshing and renewing him in spite of the day's harassments, that it is easy for the average person to tell there is something genuinely different about his life.

Ask the Holy Spirit to impart His power and presence to you today, in this very hour. Pray for Him to help you in the ways you need Him most — to shine like a diamond under water!

Eternal Possibilities

Lord, what is man, that You take
knowledge of him? Or the son of man,
that You are mindful of him?
Psalm 144:3 (NKJV)

Among collectors there is always a demand for items bearing the signature of a master craftsman. A stamp on the bottom of a vase indicates it was made by Wedgwood, a label on a violin authenticates a genuine Stradivarius, giving to each item a value far above others. In each case, the potter or the violin maker has established a reputation for excellence in craftsmanship. Anything that bears their names is considered very valuable.

Human beings were made by a great craftsman, the Lord God, our Creator. The psalmist gives praise to God for the magnificence of his own physical being, "I will praise You, for I am fearfully and wonderfully made" (Psalm 139:14 NKJV). Of all God's creatures, only men and women bear the image and likeness of God. That quality separates us from every other creature. We alone are made to fellowship with Him for eternity.

In his essay *The Weight of Glory*, C. S. Lewis wrote about the potential destiny of each human being:

> "*It is a serious thing...to remember that the dullest and most uninteresting person you can talk to may one day be a creature which, if you saw it now, you would be strongly tempted to worship, or else a horror and a corruption such as you now meet, if at all, only in a nightmare. All day long we are, in some degree, helping each other to one or other of these destinations. It is in the light of these overwhelming possibilities...that we conduct all our dealings with one another, all friendships, all loves, all play, all politics. There are no ordinary people. You have never talked to a mere mortal. Nations, cultures, arts, civilisations — these are mortal, and their life is to ours as the life of a gnat. But it is immortals whom we joke with, work with, marry, snub, and exploit — immortal horrors or everlasting splendours.*"[10]

Is Anyone Out There?

*Let your light shine before men, that they may see your good
deeds and praise your Father in heaven.*
Matthew 5:16 (NIV)

One of the biggest complaints some of us have
about life today is the feeling that we have more
interaction with machines than we do with people.
Ever since computers became essential business tools
and television became the entertainment center in
most homes, it's been getting harder to have
meaningful human contact in our daily lives. It's even
more difficult to find someone who will go out of his
way to do something kind for a person he's never met.

When a uniform factory in the Midwest closed its
doors for what was presumably the last time, one of its
customers did just that. As the factory workers were facing
certain unemployment in their small town, this gentleman
decided to buy and reopen the plant. Needless to say, the
workers were amazed, pleased, and disbelieving.

The man, a native Midwesterner who owned several uniform shops on the West Coast, had come into a large fortune. He believed that if your cup was full and running over, you should share your blessings with others. When he tried to place an order and found out that the uniform factory had gone out of business, he decided to put his philosophy into action.

The customer bought the factory and started putting people back to work. He provided his employees with their first health plan, jazzed up the uniform styles to make them more attractive to buyers, began replacing outdated machinery, and made other improvements to the plant.[11]

Do you have to be rich to bring a ray of sunshine into someone's life? Not at all! Sometimes money is involved in making a meaningful change, but it's the person who signs the check and his desire to do something good that is behind it.

No matter how much or how little we have, we can each do something to make someone else's path a little smoother.

Circadian Meetings

To everything there is a season,
a time for every purpose under heaven.
Ecclesiastes 3:1 (NKJV)

A business consultant once advised executives to follow this pattern for scheduling their meetings and appointments:

- Have breakfast meetings to set agendas, give assignments, and introduce new projects.

- Have lunch meetings to negotiate deals, give advice to key staff members, and discuss midcourse corrections.

- Have afternoon meetings to interview prospective employees, clients, or vendors, to return phone calls, and to resolve personnel issues.

From this consultant's perspective, morning hours are best spent in task activities, midday hours in problem-solving, and afternoon hours are best devoted to people-intensive activities. The reason has little to do with management and much to do with biology. Our "circadian rhythms" seem to put us at a high-energy time in the morning, and a low-energy time in the afternoon. Meeting with people requires less energy than attention to task and detail.

This afternoon, perhaps you can meet a friend or invite colleagues into your office for a bit of refreshment and conversation. Schedule relationship-building meetings in the afternoon. Take time out for a brief end-of-the-day conversation with a secretary or another person who works under your supervision. Allow time for light conversation and share about personal matters — such as the antics of a toddler or accomplishments of a teen in the family.

Jesus no doubt spent full days in ministry, preaching, teaching, and healing those who flocked to Him. But at the close of His ministry-intensive hours, Jesus spent time with his friends. We are not only wise to follow His example — it appears to be the way we were created!

Playtime!

Blessed be the Lord your God,
who delighted in you.
1 Kings 10:9 (NKJV)

*D*o you remember how you felt when you were a child and the final bell of the school day sounded? Freedom! Time to play!

For most children, the time immediately following school is a time for:

- unstructured fun — no more assignments to be completed in a specific class period,

- noise and activity — no more restrictions to sit still and be quiet,

- friendships — no more working on your own to read a book or complete an assignment, and

- games — *work*books are left behind and *home*work is yet to come.

What ever happened to those good ol' days? you may ask. Perhaps it is time to recapture them.

Build in a little playtime at the end of your work day. Let it be unstructured. Allow yourself to be a little noisy. Move about and flex those tired muscles. Spend a little time with friends. Play a game — perhaps handball with a colleague, a set of tennis with a friend, or a game of hopscotch with your child.

We all know the saying, "All work and no play makes for a very dull day." Believe it! Not only will the day be dull, but you are likely to be dull.

The Lord made you with a capacity for fun, with an ability to smile and laugh, a desire to kick up your heels and frolic a bit, and a need for freedom of motion. He created the world for you to enjoy — and to enjoy it with Him!

The Scriptures say that the Lord "delights" in us. Could it be that the Lord delights in what delights us? Could it be that the Lord desires to have someone with whom to have complete fellowship, including someone with whom to laugh, play, and relax?

Could it be? Why not find out today!

The Sympathetic Jewel

But I say unto you, Love your enemies, bless them that curse you, do good to them that hate you, and pray for them which despitefully use you, and persecute you.

Matthew 5:44

Have you ever noticed that those who reject you often seem to lack joy. They could be guarded and standoffish because they have been rejected themselves. Their rejection of you may be a defense mechanism.

Sometimes your warm attitude toward them can make all the difference. This is illustrated by the story of a man who visited a jewelry store owned by a friend. His friend showed him magnificent diamonds and other splendid stones. Among these stones the visitor spotted one that seemed quite lusterless. Pointing to it, he said, "That stone has no beauty at all."

His friend put the gem in the hollow of his hand and closed his fingers tightly around it. In a few moments, he uncurled his fingers.

What a surprise! The entire stone gleamed with the splendor of a rainbow. "What have you done to it?" asked the astonished man.

His friend answered, "This is an opal. It is what we call the sympathetic jewel. It only needs to be gripped with the human hand to bring out its full beauty."

People are very much like opals. Without warmth, they become dull and colorless. But "grasp" them with the warmth and love of God and they come alive with personality and humor. Unlike chameleons who simply adapt to their background, people who feel embraced by the love of God and His people come alive with colorful personalities all their own.

It's difficult to embrace those who have rejected us. However, if we can see beyond the facade they have erected to the potential inside them, we can be the healing hands of Jesus extended to them...and bring healing to ourselves in the process.

What's the Rush?

Be patient, then, brothers, until the Lord's coming.
James 5:7 (NIV)

Rush-hour traffic. What comes to mind when you hear those words? Chances are they don't put a smile on your face, cause your heartbeat to slow or your blood pressure to drop to healthy levels. More likely, they bring up images of exhaust smoke, angry drivers, brake lights, and those ever-popular "Detour" or "Lane Closed Ahead" signs.

"Rush-hour" has become an oxymoron, like "jumbo shrimp." Too many cars have taken the "rush" out of "rush hour." Despite the number of people working part-time, on late shifts, or at home, more cars seem to be on the road between 8:00 and 9:00 a.m. and 5:00 and 6:00 p.m. than there are people on the planet. And we all know there's absolutely nothing that can be done about it — unless you live in Thailand.

What's the Rush?

Proving that traffic cops have a sense of humor, an officer in Bangkok gave his men some rather unusual instructions. During morning rush hour at one of the worst spots in town, these traffic directors suddenly looked more like dance-troupe hopefuls than ticket-writing law enforcers.

Since the traffic wasn't going anywhere anyway, why not do some pirouettes or some break dancing? Why not smile at frustrated motorists? Why not lighten the mood (if not the load) on the road?

The result has been all they hoped. The traffic is still tied up in knots, but people are more cheerful about their situation, and the cops are happier too.[12]

Sometimes we feel pressed on all sides, and there seems to be no way out. Perhaps those around us keep turning up the heat, and we can sense we're getting closer and closer to the breaking point.

That's when we need to realize how far we've already come, and that the rest of the journey will have bright moments if we'll only reach out for them. That's the time to laugh *anyway* and do a few pirouettes!

The Tea Cart

Be kind to one another, tenderhearted.
Ephesians 4:32 (NKJV)

A number of years ago, a corporation experimented with the recommendation of one of its vice-presidents. At three o'clock each afternoon for a month, a tea cart pushed by a maid in uniform mysteriously appeared on the executive floor. The cart was laden with fine china and linen napkins, as well as silver urns and trays of simple but elegant sweets. Executives and their secretaries and administrative assistants were invited to come out of their offices and from behind their desks to select a flavor of tea and a sweet treat from the cart.

Moments of pleasantry and conversation followed naturally. In many cases, people who had worked on the executive floor for years met their colleagues for the first time or became better acquainted with them. The tea cart stayed for thirty minutes and then was pushed away quietly.

❀ · ❀ · ❀ · ❀ · ❀ · ❀ · ❀ · ❀ · ❀ · ❀ · ❀ · ❀ · ❀

After a month, the president of the company conducted an informal poll among those who had enjoyed a "month of tea." He discovered that, without exception, each person reported a new air of civility on the floor. Many employees commented on how much they had enjoyed the tea break and on how they felt this service had increased morale.

Encouraged by such positive results, the president ordered a "tea cart" service for each of the floors in the corporate building. The same benefits were noted by all of the employees. Shortly thereafter, the service company noted an increase in customer satisfaction, and in its wake a significant rise in profit. Although no one was so bold as to say a tea cart impacted profit...could that be the case?

A kind word, a kind deed, a kind attitude — they all speak volumes. They impact the way we think of ourselves and others, which impacts the way we work. The apostle Paul certainly knew this to be true when he advised, "Be of good comfort, be of one mind, live in peace; and the God of love and peace will be with you" (2 Corinthians 13:11 NKJV).

The Stranger's Voice

But when the morning was now come, Jesus stood on the shore:
but the disciples knew not that it was Jesus.
John 21:4

Some years ago at a resort area along the East Coast, a small community was having an open town meeting about some financial problems they were facing. Among the two dozen or more in attendance was one man no one recognized — a visitor who had apparently dropped in for the meeting. The discussion focused on the desperate state of the town's coffers and on possible ways to raise funds.

During the discussion, the stranger attempted several times to make a comment about various projects being considered, but each time he was interrupted. Eventually, he quit trying and left the hall.

Just as the unknown visitor exited, someone arriving late came into the hall. Out of breath from hurrying, the late-comer asked, "What was he doing here? Is he going to help us?"

The rest asked, "Who are you talking about?"

He said, "You mean you don't know? That was John D. Rockefeller who just left the hall. His yacht is in our harbor. Didn't you get his help?"

In despair someone replied, "No, we didn't get his help. We didn't know who he was."

This true story illustrates two key points:

First, good manners will always have their rewards and rudeness its price.

Second, this story reminds us that we may become so busy trying to find the solution to a problem, we may drown out the voice of the Master who has *all* solutions among His vast resources.

When you are faced with a difficult problem, listen first to what Jesus says to you. No other opinion or solution can ever yield more positive results than His!

Help Others, Help Yourself

For as the body without the spirit is dead,
so faith without works is dead also.
James 2:26

A tornado rips through a southern town and destroys most of the buildings in its path. Those that remain standing have sustained serious damage, but the owners can't make all of the repairs.

A church in the South has a small congregation, and an even smaller budget. Expenses are met each week, but the funds aren't there to hire someone to do minor but much needed repairs.

Who comes to the rescue? A group of mostly retirees in recreational vehicles. They travel throughout the South during the autumn and winter months, escaping cold temperatures and doing good along the way. Some are experienced in carpentry and construction and some are not, but they all have the same goal: to make their time count by helping others.

Help Others, Help Yourself

The United Methodist Church chooses projects and assigns teams to each site. The workers, who pay all their expenses, meet at the appointed time and get right to work. To keep the jobs enjoyable, everyone works four days and then has three days off to relax and see the sights. The fun part, reported one woman volunteer, is the opportunity to have fellowship with like-minded people.[13]

The same generosity of spirit, on a slightly different scale, is described in the Book of Acts. "All the believers were one in heart and mind. No one claimed that any of his possessions was his own, but they shared everything they had. There were no needy persons among them. For from time to time those who owned lands or houses sold them, brought the money from the sales and put it at the apostles' feet, and it was distributed to anyone as he had need" (Acts 4:32,34-35 NIV).

When we have the chance to do good, we should jump at it. "So in everything, do to others what you would have them do to you, for this sums up the Law and the Prophets," Jesus said in Matthew 7:12 (NIV). Jesus asked us to serve, and we will be blessed when we do so.

Opposites Balanced

*The day is Yours, the night also is Yours; You have
prepared the light and the sun. You have set all the
borders of the earth; You have made summer and winter.*
Psalm 74:16-17 (NKJV)

*M*uch of our life seems to be suspended
between opposites. We grow up learning to label
things as good and bad, hurtful and helpful, naughty
and nice. People are kind or mean. The thermostat can
be adjusted to avoid extremes of heat and cold. We
look forward to the changing of seasons from summer
to winter. Time is divided by day and night.

Not only are these opposites helpful to us in
defining or "bordering" our lives, but they can also
help us release stress.

Very often people who are engaged in physical,
muscle-intensive work all day choose a "mental"
activity with which to relax and unwind. Those who
have idea-intensive jobs often enjoy relaxing with

hobbies that make use of their hands, such as wood carving or needlework. Those in sterile, well-ordered environments look forward to coming home to weed their gardens.

Structured tasks and routines are good relaxation for those involved in the creative arts. The musician runs home to his computer. The surgeon delights in growing orchids in a hothouse. The factory worker enjoys crossword puzzles. The executive unwinds in the kitchen, preparing gourmet meals.

The Lord created us for this rhythm of opposites. God told Noah as he and his family left the ark that Noah would experience "seedtime and harvest, cold and heat, winter and summer, and day and night shall not cease" (Genesis 8:22 NKJV). Mankind was set in a world of opposites.

When you feel stressed out at day's end, try engaging in an activity that is opposite in nature to the work you have been doing. If you have been using your mind, turn to an activity that is physical. If you have been exerting physical energy, turn to an activity that is mental.

Let the pendulum swing back to rest in a central location!

A Little Ceremony, Please

And ye shall find rest unto your souls.
Matthew 11:29

*A*fternoon tea at London's Ritz Hotel is described as the last delicious morsel of Edwardian London. Helen Simpson offers this description in The London Ritz Book of Afternoon Tea:

"*I*n the elegantly columned Palm Court, the light is kind, the cakes are frivolous and the tempo is calm, confident and leisurely. Takers of tea perch on rose-coloured Louis XVI chairs at marble tables, sipping their steaming cups of tea....There are no clocks, and although it is just possible to glimpse the flash of Piccadilly's taxis and buses if you look hard in the direction of the doors, a strange sense of taking a holiday from time heightens the pleasure of taking tea here. People look more beautiful than they do in real life due to the flattering lighting. Here is one of the few places outside church...where a woman may wear a hat and feel entirely at ease....Those approaching the Palm Court clad in such garments as

*jeans, shorts or sneakers will be reluctantly turned away
— and no one is admitted without a reservation. The
dark tea leaves are steeping in boiling water when
brought to the table with a selection of tiny finger
sandwiches, scones and cakes."*[14]

Why all that fuss over a cup of tea and a snack?
Because the "ceremony" of drinking afternoon tea
provides more refreshment than the food and drink
alone can deliver. It requires the participants to cease
all other activities for a short period of time, take in a
little sustenance, and give attention to others who are
sharing the repast. It is an opportunity for one to put
down whatever knotty problems have been occupying
the day thus far and take up lighter issues for a few
minutes. The body gets refreshment and rest (no one
stands for tea) and the mind gets a little vacation.

Tea time also provides a natural opportunity for
the spirit to be refreshed. Taking tea alone gives one the
chance to reflect on the ups and downs of the day in
quiet prayer, receiving fuel to move confidently
through the rest of the day.

If you are "taking tea" with a friend or friends, why
not share one thing that God has done for each of you.
Praise at tea time gives a new meaning to the phrase
"high tea!"

⚜ · ⚜ · ⚜ · ⚜ · ⚜ · ⚜ · ⚜ · ⚜ · ⚜ · ⚜ · ⚜ · ⚜ · ⚜

Hippos

Then God saw everything that He had made,
and indeed it was very good.
Genesis 1:31 (NKJV)

When we think of a hippopotamus, the word "graceful" rarely comes to mind. Rather, we are likely to think of the words "cumbersome," "ugly," and "distorted." There is little to admire in the way a hippo looks or acts...or so we think. They seem to be large, rocklike masses, ready to tip over any unsuspecting boat that may pass too close.

Visitors to a new exhibit at a popular zoo are learning otherwise, however. A large glass aquarium gives visitors an opportunity to watch hippos from a different vantage point — under water.

They are surprised to discover that even with its short fat legs, bulky body, and oversized head, the hippopotamus is a very graceful, agile, and strong swimmer, capable of staying under water for long periods of time. The tiny eyes of the hippo are better adapted to the underwater murkiness of African rivers than to bright sunlight. Indeed, the hippo spends much of its time foraging along the bottoms of rivers.

The main function of the hippo in the natural order appears to be that of "channel clearer." Hippos eat enormous amounts of river grasses that grow along the banks of rivers, thus keeping the river free of blockages that might cause floods.

Ugly? Yes. But hippos are gifted in unusual ways and have a valuable role to play.

Every day you will encounter people who may seem awkward, different, ugly, or without much purpose. Look again! God has created each element of nature — plant, mineral, bird, fish, and animal — to fulfill a specific purpose, and to do so with unique talents and abilities. There is an element of beauty, gracefulness, and goodness in everything He creates.

On A Clear Day

For you will go out with joy, and be led forth with peace; the mountains and the hills will break forth into shouts of joy before you, and all the trees of the field will clap their hands.
Isaiah 55:12 (NASB)

Ask any person who exercises on a regular basis, and he will tell you that the benefits of a good workout go far beyond the physical. Many people end their work day with a trip to the gym. Doing so helps them to clear their head of the day's frustrations, gives them more energy to face the evening ahead, calms them down, and improves their mood. It is also a complete departure from sitting at a desk all day.

While any exercise can be helpful, research has shown that *where* you exercise can make a big difference in the benefits derived from a workout session. A psychologist at an East Coast university tracked hormonal and mood changes in a group of runners who participated in three different jogs:

- outdoors,

- indoors, on a treadmill, while listening to "sounds of nature" tapes, and

- indoors, on a treadmill, while listening to a tape of their own heartbeat.

Can you guess which jog proved to be the most beneficial? The outdoor jog. Levels of positive mood hormones (adrenaline and noradrenaline) were up, while stress hormone (cortisol) levels were down in those who had exercised outside.

It's not just your heart that's affected by exercise; so is your head. If your brain is bored or feeling stress, you won't get the best effect from your workout. In fact, you're more likely to quit.

It seems environment really matters. Whether you're exercising or just taking a few moments to relax with a cup of tea, where you do it can be nearly as important as why and how you do it. Find a delightful, stimulating spot for your getaway, and make the most of your break.

As children, we often asked our neighborhood friends, "Can you come out and play?" It's still a good question to ask!

A Time for Everything

There is a right time for everything.
Ecclesiastes 3:1 (TLB)

Most Christians are familiar with the passage in Ecclesiastes that tells us, "To everything there is a season." Consider this modern-day version of the same message:

To everything there is a time...

A time to wind up, and a time to wind down;

A time to make the call, and a time to unplug the phone;

A time to set the alarm, and a time to sleep in;

A time to get going, and a time to let go.

A time for starting new projects, and a time for celebrating victories;

A time for employment, and a time for retirement;

A time for overtime, and a time for vacation;

A time for making hay, and a time for lying down on a stack of it to watch the clouds go by.

A time for making plans, and a time for implementing them;

A time for seeing the big picture, and a time for mapping out details;

A time for working alone, and a time for involving others.

A time for building morale, and a time for growing profits;

A time for giving incentives, and a time for granting rewards;

A time for giving advice, and a time for taking it.

No matter what your situation or environment, the Lord has designed a rhythm for life that includes rest and exertion. If you maintain this balance, you'll likely find there is plenty of "time for everything" that is truly beneficial to you!

The Miracle of a Kind Word

For thou hast lifted me up, and hast
not made my foes to rejoice over me.
Psalm 30:1

The Reverend Purnell Bailey tells of a convict from Darlington, England, who had just been released from prison. He had spent three long years in prison for embezzlement, and though he wanted to return to his hometown, he was concerned about the social ostracism and possible ridicule he might have to endure from some of the townsfolk. Still, he was lonesome for his home and decided to risk the worst.

He had barely set foot on the main street of town when he encountered the mayor himself.

"Hello!" greeted the mayor in a cheery voice. "I'm glad to see you! How are you?" The man appeared ill at ease and so the mayor moved on.

Years later, the former mayor and the ex-convict accidentally met in another town. The latter said, "I want you to know what you did for me when I came out of prison."

"What did I do?" asked the mayor.

"You spoke a kind word to me and changed my life," replied the grateful man.[15]

We cannot always know how important the seed of a kind word may be to the one who receives it. More often than we know, words of encouragement or recognition provide a turning point in a person's outlook on life.

Just as Jesus spoke with love and acceptance to the hated tax collector Zaccheus, the mayor set the tone for others' contacts with the ex-convict by openly and warmly addressing him as a neighbor. People watch those they respect for cues regarding their own relationships with certain people.

Genuine, kind words cost the giver nothing but can mean the world to the one receiving them.

Today, don't be put off when someone to whom you offer a kind word seems uncomfortable or embarrassed. Recognize they may be unpracticed at receiving your love and compassion, even though they need it greatly.

Simple Pleasures

His soul shall dwell at ease.
Psalm 25:13

There are many ways to enjoy tea time — formal, casual, business, cream teas, Christmas tea, tea served in a mug, tea presented in a fine china cup, a picnic tea outdoors in the country, a cozy, snuggled-up-beside-the-fireplace tea for two, an elegant tea on the lawn, or an hour of culinary delight in a stylish tea room.

Briton Aubrey Franklin was appointed "Tea Ambassador" to America by the Tea Council of the U.S.A. to instruct Americans in the proper use of tea. He recollects his memories of childhood tea times in England:

> *When I was a young lad, teatime was that special hour for sharing stories and having a giggle or two with my family. These everyday gatherings, enhanced by the ritual of teatime, helped us to feel united. To be able to chat about the humorous and oftimes tremulous events of the day was*

not only cathartic, but enabled us to know and enjoy each
other. This is what is needed today, a time set aside for the
specific purpose of sharing not only tea and its delicious
accompaniments, but love....Instead of friends and families
tuning out by immediately switching on the telly, start
tuning in to one another again. Teatime is the perfect time
and is a most delightfully exhilarating habit."[16]

Life's simple pleasures are those we most frequently ignore — often in pursuit of greater and grander schemes of happiness.

However you choose to do it, try to set aside some casual time to spend with a friend or loved one for no other reason than to relax and enjoy a laugh, rekindle intimacy, help soothe each other's jangled nerves, or just to let your minds wander together among uncharted dreams.

Accessibility

A man who has friends must himself be friendly.
Proverbs 18:24 (NKJV)

*T*he end of a work day is a time when you may find it very pleasant and beneficial to make yourself a little more accessible to other people.

If you have had a "closed-door, nose-to-the-grindstone" attitude all day...now may be the time to open the door.

If you've been on the phone for what seems like hours, now may be the time to wander the halls and have a brief face-to-face conversation with a colleague or someone you supervise.

If you have felt bogged down with paperwork or glued to a computer screen, now may be the time to walk to the cafeteria and get an energizing snack. Invite someone to go with you or meet you there for a few minutes of casual conversation.

If you have been indoors with children or house chores, it might be time to call a neighborhood friend and go for a walk.

Robert Fulghum has written: "The grass is not, in fact, always greener on the other side of the fence. Fences have nothing to do with it. The grass is greenest where it is watered."

Every day, regardless of our environment or situation, we need to have human contact and communication. God built this need into us, and from the story of God's relationship with Adam and Eve in the Garden of Eden, we can assume that God enjoyed a late-in-the-day stroll with His creation — a time of sharing lives, not simply working together on tasks.

Share with others in a heart-to-heart way. Listen with open ears to the feelings a person may be expressing, even more closely than you listen to the details of their story. Be willing to help carry their burdens and rejoice at their victories. Allow yourself to be vulnerable to others in return — revealing your own wounds, concerns, worries, frustrations, hopes, dreams, and desires. Accessibility is the first key to genuine relationship.

You're All Heart

Come to me, all you that are weary and are
carrying heavy burdens, and I will give you rest.
Matthew 11:28 (NRSV)

That twinge in your chest and that pain in your arm...is it just a muscle pull or is it something more serious, such as a heart problem? If it is your heart, what caused the problem and what can you do to fix it?

When you consult your doctor, one of the first things he might ask is what kind of stress you are experiencing in your life. Most of us would answer, "Too much of the wrong kind." After all, it's not easy to cope with each day's major and minor irritations, people who annoy us, and events beyond our control.

In our world, stress is here to stay and many of us have heart problems (or loved ones who do). So how can we help ourselves?

Surgery and medication aren't always the answer. And, believe it or not, diet and exercise aren't necessarily the most important factors in restoring your heart's health. Studies have shown that having a spouse or other loved one to talk to and rely on, avoiding the traps of depression and anxiety, and having a sense that you can make a positive change in your condition can overcome the effects of even the most seriously blocked arteries.[17]

How often do we worry about things we can't do anything about? "Do not worry about tomorrow," Jesus said. "For tomorrow will worry about itself" (Matthew 6:34 NIV).

How often do we see ourselves as powerless? Remember what the Lord told Paul: "My grace is sufficient for you, for My strength is made perfect in weakness" (2 Corinthians 12:9 NKJV).

How often have we succumbed to depression and avoided contact with our spouse or a friend? Paul told the early church, "Therefore encourage one another and build each other up" (1 Thessalonians 5:11 NIV).

We each have a part to play in our own physical and spiritual restoration and in the restoration of others. With God's help and the support of our brothers and sisters in the Lord, we can have healthy hearts.

Coping with Rush Hour

*See then that you walk circumspectly, not as fools
but as wise, redeeming the time!*
Ephesians 5:15-16 (NKJV)

One of the best ways to cope with rush-hour traffic is simply to avoid it!

If your work environment allows for flex time, consider taking that option. You may need a few weeks to adjust your inner clock so that you arrive at work by 6:00 a.m., but you are likely to delight in returning home by 3:00 p.m. In addition, the commute to and from work is likely to take far less time and be far less stressful.

Your work situation may allow you to use a home office, communicating with colleagues by fax, phone, or modem. Those who discipline themselves to work well at home usually enjoy the experience and often find they get more accomplished during "at home" days than during "office" days.

Coping with Rush Hour

If you can't avoid the rush hour and your commute is a long one, there are several things you can do to make the journey to and from the office less stressful. First, think comfort in your clothing. Put on ties, jewelry, and other accessories after arriving at work, and remove them before you start home. Keep comfortable shoes in your car.

Engage your mind in something totally unrelated to work, home, or the traffic, such as favorite music or a teaching tape. Consider a motivational or inspirational message on the way to work and a spiritually-oriented message when you come home.

Think of your commute as an appointment you make with yourself and the Lord. Plan to enjoy those minutes alone with Him, in conversation with the One who is truly the captain, pilot, and chauffeur of your life. Talk to Him. Listen. Let Him commute with you. If your mind is on Him, you will be far less likely to feel "rushed" when the traffic in front of you comes to a complete stop!

Our Everything

Christ is all, and is in all.
Colossians 3:11 (NIV)

World famous orchestra conductor Arturo Toscanini was very exacting and almost tyrannical in rehearsals, but the musicians who played with him and his audiences never doubted his focus.

To prepare for a performance of Beethoven's Ninth Symphony, he rehearsed each section of instruments separately. They played their parts over and over again until he was satisfied. Finally the sections were joined together.

The date arrived for the performance of this master symphony. The orchestra performed superbly, inspired by Toscanini's demanding artistic leadership. At the close of the concert, the first violinist said to the musician next to him, "If he scolds us after that I will jump up and push him off the platform."

Our Everything

Toscanini did not scold the musicians nor critique their performance in any way. Instead he stood silent, arms outstretched, his deep-set eyes burning with an inner fire, the light of a great rapture upon his face, and a spirit of utter contentment enfolding him. After a long silence, he said, "Who am I? Who is Toscanini? Who are you? I am nobody! You are nobody!"

The crowded concert hall was hushed. The master conductor remained with his arms extended and the audience and orchestra waited in awe. Then, his face beaming with the light of one who has seen a vision, he added, "Beethoven is everything — EVERYTHING!"[18]

There are times in our life when we become aware of our smallness and God's overwhelming greatness. His magnificence is not the kind that pulls us down so He can be exalted at our expense. His majesty motivates and calls us to higher standards and inspires us to serve noble purposes.

This afternoon when you sit quietly with your tea, ponder the greatness of God, the beautiful sacrifice of His Son Jesus, and the gentle power of His Holy Spirit within you. Let Him be everything to you!

Brewing Good Relationships

A word fitly spoken is like apples
of gold in settings of silver.
Proverbs 25:11 (NKJV)

*M*ost tea-drinkers would never consider tossing a tea bag in the nearest cup of hot water as the proper way to make a cup of tea. When one wants the best pot of tea, there are several rules for brewing that will assure the tea is a treat for the palate.

Always choose teas whose basic flavors are pleasing to you or your guests. If they are loose teas, don't be afraid to do a little blending, measuring one teaspoon per cup plus one teaspoon per pot. Let the tea steep for several minutes but don't boil tea leaves. If you do, bitter tannins will emerge.

Like brewing tea, forming good relationships takes time and attention to be satisfying. Here are ten ways to show the love of Jesus to others — guaranteed to bring out the best "flavor" of each person:

Brewing Good Relationships

1. Speak to people. There is nothing as nice as a cheerful word of greeting.

2. Smile at people. It takes 72 muscles to frown; 14 to smile.

3. Call people by name. The sweetest music is the sound of one's own name.

4. Be friendly and helpful.

5. Be cordial. Speak and act as if everything you do is a pleasure.

6. Be genuinely interested in people. You can like everybody if you try.

7. Be generous with praise — cautious with criticism.

8. Be considerate of the feelings of others. It will be appreciated.

9. Be thoughtful of the opinions of others.

10. Be alert to give service. What counts most in life is what we do for others.[19]

These things take time, but like the time spent perfecting that pot of tea, it is well worth the extra effort.

The Spinning Wheel

Don't let the world around you
squeeze you into its own mold.
Romans 12:2 *(PHILLIPS)*

In Ordering Your Private World, Gordon MacDonald tells the story of Mohandas Gandhi, the Hindu leader who was known as "India's George Washington" by leading his people to national independence. People who have read biographies of Gandhi or have seen his life portrayed in film are often impressed by his calm and serene character.

Gandhi frequently was found among the poor and diseased in India's cities. He would walk among them offering a touch of hope, a word of encouragement, or a gentle affirming smile. The next day Gandhi might be found in palaces and government buildings negotiating with the most powerful and educated men of his age.

How did he keep a balanced sense of self in these vast extremes of Indian society? How did he maintain humility when the great masses of people cheered him as a hero or he was summoned to talk with kings and government leaders?

Gandhi spun the wool from which his clothes were made. When he returned to his simple dwelling, he sat on the floor to spin wool on his spinning wheel. This simple chore restored to him a sense of who he was and what was basic, practical, and essential to life. It helped him to resist the public acclaim that might distort who he knew himself to be or distract him from the purpose he believed was his destiny.[20]

We each need to make an intentional effort in our lives to remain true to our deepest selves, that part of us which is created in God's image and designed to bring Him glory. Often we structure our lives around the activities in which we participate. But the Lord calls us to order our lives around His priorities and purposes. Then we can be His people in the world, but not of the world.

A Pastor's Heart

Guard what was committed to your trust.
1 Timothy 6:20 (NKJV)

A manager with a major corporation once heard a visiting preacher say: "If you have any type of supervisor's role in your company, then you need to have a pastor's heart. You need to minister to those people just as you would expect your pastor to minister to you."

The preacher made a clear differentiation between being a preacher of sermons and being a "pastor" to the people. He described a pastor as a loving shepherd who made sure all the sheep in the parish were nurtured.

The words lodged in the executive's heart. He had never thought of himself as a pastor before — far from it! His was a factory environment where tough discipline was expected from him...or so he thought. Nevertheless, the idea of having a pastor's heart was one he couldn't shake.

A Pastor's Heart

❀ · ❀ · ❀ · ❀ · ❀ · ❀ · ❀ · ❀ · ❀ · ❀ · ❀ · ❀

The executive began to think about what his own pastor did — visiting bedsides and funeral homes, conducting home visitations, extending Christian friendship and concern. He decided that a portion of each day would be spent doing the same.

With increasing frequency, he visited relatives of his employees who were hospitalized. He made it a point to ask about family members and to show up at special occasions, from little league playoffs to graduation ceremonies. He began to encourage employees in as many ways as possible.

What he discovered was that morale improved greatly in his area of the factory, and along with it productivity and quality. In his own life, he found much greater satisfaction in managing with a pastor's heart than with an iron fist!

John Henry Newman once wrote:

I sought to hear the voice of God
And climbed the topmost steeple,
But God declared: "Go down again —
I dwell among the people."

Read the Book

Listen to counsel and receive instruction.
Proverbs 19:20 (NKJV)

*T*wo women who were having lunch together in an elegant, gourmet restaurant decided to end their repast with a cup of tea. The tea arrived and was poured into exquisite china teacups, but after taking the first sip one woman complained to the waiter. "Sir, this tastes like benzene. Are you sure it's tea?"

The waiter replied, "Oh yes, it must be. The coffee tastes like turpentine."

If you are serving a pot of tea, you will have good results with this recipe:

1. Rinse out the teakettle and start with fresh, cold tap water. Never boil anything but water in your teakettle.

2. Bring the water to its first rolling boil. Never overboil! Overboiling takes the oxygen out of the water, which in turn creates a flat beverage.

3. Take the teapot to the teakettle and rinse out the pot with the boiling water from the kettle. Never take the kettle to the teapot, as you lose one degree of heat per second. Water for tea must be 212 degrees.

4. Use one teabag or teaspoon of loose tea per cup. Leaves enter the warm teapot and the infusion begins when the leaf opens.

5. Pour hot water gently over the leaves. (Never bruise the leaves.)

6. Allow the tea to brew for three to five minutes, according to the blend of tea and how strong you like it.[21]

Following the instructions of connoisseurs can help us make a good cup of tea. The same is true to in living a good life!

The Bible is God's instruction book: "All Scripture is given by inspiration of God, and is profitable for doctrine, for reproof, for correction, for instruction in righteousness" (2 Timothy 3:16 NKJV). We are wise to follow its instructions!

The Grand Finale

For the vision is yet for an appointed time;
but at the end it will speak...though it tarries,
wait for it; because it will surely come.
Habakkuk 2:3 (NKJV)

*M*any of the major symphonies we know and love have what has come to be called "a grand finale." Beethoven's symphonies, in particular, are noted for this. The final movement of the symphony may begin with a gentle and melodious theme, then suddenly there will be a flurry of sound and rhythm that builds, increasing to a climax that often includes a great deal of percussion and every section of the orchestra playing at full tilt. The listener is swept toward a glorious conclusion.

Most projects, and most work days, follow a similar pattern. We may call it "momentum," but at 4:00 or 5:00 p.m. we find ourselves shifting into high gear to accomplish everything listed on our agenda.

The closer we get to completion of a project, the greater energy we pour into it and the more we are focused. Our work output during the final hour of the day — or the final segment of a project — may be many times more.

Rather than attempt to change this dynamic, go with the flow of it! Enhance the process by giving yourself a tea time, when you can put your feet up for a few seconds and enjoy a little nourishment. Use these quiet moments to regroup, rethink, replan, refocus.

Consider carefully what you *must* do in the final hour of the day and what can be set aside. Let the advice of the Scriptures ring true in your spirit: "God will take care of your tomorrow, too. Live one day at a time" (Matthew 6:34 TLB).

Jesus' final three years of ministry were intense and eternally meaningful. They were preceded by at least 25 years of preparation. Take time to rejuvenate yourself before your grand finale!

Tempest in a Teapot

For all the promises of God in Him are Yes,
and in Him Amen, to the glory of God through us.
2 Corinthians 1:20 (NKJV)

*H*ave you had a tempest in a teapot kind of day? Perhaps you are disoriented by a bad night's sleep, distressed over the phone call from your child's teacher, or pressured by the impending review by your boss. On days like that it's easy to erupt into a storm over the least trifling matter. Times like that become opportunities to say "yes" to God.

In her book *Diamonds in the Dust*, Joni Eareckson Tada asks, "Do you remember when you said 'yes' to Jesus? How long ago was it? A few months, maybe years? I said 'yes' to the Lord in November 1964 when I was a teenager. But I also said 'yes' to Him just the other day."

Tada describes a day when she had a quarrel with her husband Ken. To escape the situation, she went with a friend to the shopping mall, where she burst out in sobs of self-pity. She said, "I couldn't hide my face in a tissue, and my wheelchair was too big for me to escape behind several clothes racks. All I could do was sit there, cry, and stare at the mannequins with the plastic smiles."

Trying to recover from waves of sobs, she said aloud what she had said many times before, "Yes, Jesus, I choose you. I don't choose self-pity or resentment. I say 'yes' to you!"

With her face still wet with tears, she felt her heart fill with peace. She said, "Nothing about my husband had changed. Shoppers on the other side of the store still picked through the racks...teenagers still ambled by, giggling and eating popcorn...but *everything* was different because of my peaceful heart. Because I said 'yes' to Jesus."[22]

We may not even know the full extent of what troubles us, but we can give our frustrations and unsettled emotions to God. "Lord, I don't understand this situation, but I know I want Your peace and Your grace to change me in the midst of this storm in my life. Thank You for caring enough about me that You gave me the desire to say 'yes' to You. Amen."

Fear Not

*Those of steadfast mind you keep in peace
— in peace because they trust in you.*
Isaiah 26:3 (NRSV)

*D*riving across the country by herself, a young woman recorded this experience:

"*I* was on the second leg of a three-leg journey, and all I wanted to do was find a motel, park the car, remove a day's accumulation of traveling dust from my weary body, and fall into bed for a good eight hours. But I couldn't stop, because I hadn't met my mileage goal for the day. I was still more than two hours from Tucumcari, New Mexico, and tired though I was, I was also bound and determined to get as close to the Texas border as I could.

"*W*hat I hadn't reckoned on was bad weather. California and Arizona had been sunny and warm, and I wrongly assumed that New Mexico in late March would hold no unpleasant surprises.

Fear Not

"*The* sun was sinking fast behind me, and soon disappeared altogether. On cross-country trips, I prefer not to drive at night — especially on unfamiliar roads — but I had a goal to meet that day, and so I pushed on.

"*A* quarter hour or so after sunset, I saw precipitation gliding past the glow of my headlights. Rain, I thought. But no, it was snow. Soon it was coming down fast and furiously at a slant, directly into my windshield, having a kaleidoscopic effect.

"*P*anic took hold. There were few cars on the interstate, no lights along the route, no parking lots to pull into and wait it out — and I could barely see the lines on the road.

"*It* wasn't the fiery furnace, but it was an ordeal I needed to work my way through. And since I couldn't see where I was going as well as I would have liked, I had to put all my faith and trust in Someone who could. I had to somehow relax in the midst of this dark, wintry valley and rely on light from another Source.

"*I* made it safely to my destination that night — not because of superior driving skills or dumb luck, but because I learned a long time ago Who it is who really keeps my car on the road."

Easy, Albert!

*A wrathful man stirreth up strife: but he
that is slow to anger appeaseth strife.*
Proverbs 15:18

Even the well controlled temper can find itself sorely tested on days when nothing seems to go according to plan. As the shadows lengthen, occasionally the fuse gets shorter.

One young father with a new baby discovered a secret to handling his temper. Desiring to take full part in the raising of his infant son, he cared for the baby on his days off, while his wife worked a part-time job. On one particular day, his son seemed to scream constantly. The father thought a visit to the park might distract the child.

He pushed the child's stroller along at an easy pace and appeared to be unruffled by his still crying baby. A mother with her baby strolled near them and she heard him speaking softly, "Easy, Albert. Control yourself."

The baby cried all the louder. "Now, now, Albert, keep your temper," he said.

Amazed at the father's calm, the mother said, "I must congratulate you on your self-control. You surely know how to speak to a baby — calmly and gently!" She patted the crying baby on the head and asked soothingly, "What's wrong, Albert?"

"No, no!" explained the father, "the baby's name is Johnny. I'm Albert!"

Albert had stumbled onto something that actually works better with adults than with babies and children. When others lose their temper or seem to be baiting you intentionally, practice speaking in your most calm, quiet voice. In most cases, your tranquil demeanor will help the other person to calm down. And practicing self-control in frustrating circumstances lengthens your own fuse — as well as diffuse strife.

Hard to do? Sure! But try this: Allow the other person to finish speaking his thoughts. Then, before you reply, take a deep breath. As you exhale say to yourself, *Jesus, I love You*. Keep it up every time you respond. The powerful name of Jesus can calm even the angriest seas of temper!

Home Free

If therefore the Son shall make you free,
you shall be free indeed.
John 8:36 (NASB)

Most of us remember hot summer nights playing the game hide-and-seek with neighborhood friends. The goal was to reach a designated point and cry "home free!" without first being detected by the person doing the seeking.

Many of us play a version of that game on a daily basis, hoping to make it home without encountering more of the world's worries and pains. We want to arrive safely and soundly where we can be nurtured by family members or friends. Home is a place we like to be completely and delightfully "free."

At home we are free to be ourselves — to talk, to praise the Lord, to show our love, to give, to receive, to relax, to do what we like to do rather than what others demand we do. These qualities certainly make home an attractive place.

There are some, however, who consider home a place where they are free to dump personal frustration, free to express anger or hostility, free to rule and reign as a bully. Such freedom doesn't quite make for a "home free" atmosphere.

To arrive home with a real "home free" attitude, dump the excess baggage of frustration, stress, and anger *before* you get home. That may mean taking time for prayer before you leave the office, or in your car. It may mean stopping by a gym to work out or staying at the office an extra hour to get your work done there rather than bringing it home.

A home that is "free" is a wonderful place. Freedom, however, must be guarded, cherished, and protected — not taken for granted or abused. We can safely reach home base to joyfully declare "Home Free!"

A Sip at a Time

My servants will sing out of the joy of their hearts.
Isaiah 65:14 (NIV)

*T*he great movie maker Cecil B. DeMille once remarked on the importance of happiness in one's life and how to savor it:

"*T*he profession one chooses to follow for a livelihood seldom brings fame and fortune, but a life lived within the dictates of one's conscience can bring happiness and satisfaction of living far beyond worldly acclaim. I expect to pass through this world but once, and any good therefore that I can do, or any kindness that I can show to any fellow creature, let me do it now. Let me not defer or neglect it, for I shall not pass this way again. Happiness must be sipped, not drained from life in great gulps — nor does it flow in a steady stream like water from a faucet. 'A portion of thyself' is a sip of happiness as satisfying as it is costless."[23]

DeMille's slow-sipping metaphor reminds us that one may sit for quite some time with a mug of hot tea resting warmly between one's hands. The warm, fragrant steam helps to revive one's attitude and generally gives a feeling of contentment. In those moments, it is easier to agree with Paul: "I have learned in whatever state I am, to be content" (Philippians 4:11 NKJV).

One of the ways in which we may experience true happiness is to "sip" from the supply of talents and abilities God gives us and use them to benefit others. "Sipping" doesn't require spending great amounts of time. Neither does it require extraordinary or professional helping skills.

Use a gift or talent you have to serve others. Volunteer for a committee at work, teach Sunday school, join a choir or musical group, coach little league, teach adults to read, or simply make an effort to get better acquainted with your colleagues.

Helen Keller, blind and deaf from the age of 19 months, had remarkable sight when it came to viewing life's priorities. She said, "Many persons have a wrong idea about what constitutes true happiness. It is not attained through self-gratification, but through fidelity to a worthy purpose."

How miraculous it is that God has built an automatic measure of happiness into every act of self-sacrifice. Take a sip of happiness by serving others!

Which Way Is Up?

I will never leave you or forsake you.
Hebrews 13:5 (NRSV)

Some years ago a speedboat driver described a harrowing racing accident from which he managed to survive. He had been nearing top speed when his boat veered slightly, striking a wave at a dangerous angle. The combined force of his speed and the size and angle of the wave sent the boat flying into the air in a dangerous spin.

The driver was thrown out of his seat and propelled deeply into the water — so deep, he had no idea which direction was "up." He had to remain calm and wait for the buoyancy of his life vest to begin pulling him toward the surface to know where it was. Then he swam quickly in that direction.

Life can put us in a tailspin at times, making us wonder, "Which way is up?" We can lose our sense of direction and the focus which keeps us on course. How do we recover our bearings?

The answer may be as simple as that discovered by the speedboat driver: Stay calm and let the "upward pull" bring you to the surface. The upward pull in our lives is that which looks beyond our finite selves to the greater reality of God.

A grandfather was taking a walk with his young granddaughter. He asked the little girl, "How far are we from home?"

The young girl answered, "Grandfather, I don't know."

"Well, do you know where you are?"

Again, seemingly unconcerned, "No, I don't know."

Then the grandfather said to her in his gentle, humorous way, "Sounds to me, honey, as if you are lost."

She looked up and said, "No, Grandfather, I can't be lost. I'm with you."

Our heavenly Father never loses sight of us and never leaves us. As long as we remain aware of His presence and are sensitive to His "upward pull," we will always know which way is up!

Rewards

Surely there is a reward for the righteous.
Psalm 58:11 (NKJV)

The writer of Hebrews encourages us to believe two things about God: First, He exists, and second, He is a "rewarder of those who diligently seek Him" (Hebrews 11:6 NKJV).

Among the rewards for those who seek the Lord are reconciliation to God, forgiveness of sins, peace of heart and mind, provision and help, and power to overcome evil. All of these are wonderful rewards...but they are also intangible ones.

Like children who live in a material world, we often desire "God with skin on." We long to see, feel, and touch our rewards. This is certainly true in the workplace. We desire the rewards of promotions, praise, and raises. It is also true at home. We long to feel appreciation, to be hugged and kissed, and to receive tangible gifts from our loved ones.

❀ · ❀ · ❀ · ❀ · ❀ · ❀ · ❀ · ❀ · ❀ · ❀ · ❀ · ❀ · ❀

Is there a link between the intangible rewards that come from God and the tangible rewards of the "real world"? There may be! Research has revealed that those who have less stress in their lives — a byproduct of peace, forgiveness, reconciliation, and spiritual power — enjoy these rewards:

- Fewer illnesses, doctor's appointments, need for medication, and overall health care expense.

- Fewer repairs on appliances and machinery. Apparently when we are at peace on the inside, we use machines with more precision and patience. We break things with less frequency.

- Fewer automobile accidents. When we are feeling peace and harmony with God and man, we are less aggressive and more careful in driving.

What *doesn't* happen to us can be just as much a reward as receiving a present or a hug. Not suffering a loss is a reward!

Diligently seek the Lord today. Make your relationship with Him your number one concern. And enjoy the rewards He will bring your way!

Know Your Objective

The man who plants and the man who waters
have one purpose, and each will be rewarded
according to his own labor.
1 Corinthians 3:8 (NIV)

In the book *Work and Contemplation* Douglas
Steere tells a story from the Great Depression era when
work was scarce, but people took great pride in
whatever job they did. Instead of receiving welfare
checks, able bodied people were given what sometimes
amounted to busywork in order to "earn" their pay.
The program was created to add a measure of dignity
to "being on the dole." Folks who did not have to take
advantage of the program openly scorned it, while the
workers who did join the program were often
embarrassed they had to do so. Steere writes:

"*Some* years ago I heard the labor expert, Whiting
Williams, tell of a squad of day laborers who were hired
one morning and put to work....The foreman...set them to

digging holes some three feet deep. When a hole was finished, it was inspected and the workman was ordered to fill it up and come to another point and to dig another hole of the same depth.

"This went on for most of the morning and finally the foreman noted the group talking in a huddle and then their spokesman came to him and said...'We're gonna quit...give us our money. You ain't gonna make fools out of us!'

"The foreman's eyes narrowed, and then understanding broke over him, and he said quietly, 'Can't you see, we're trying to find where the pipe is broken?' 'Oh,' said the man, and after a hurried word with the others...returned and said, 'Where do you want us to dig next?'"[24]

Christians are frequently admonished to value one another's work and to work in a spirit of cooperation. This is easier when every member of the team clearly understands the objective. When the objective is finally attained, each is able to share in the satisfaction of seeing his contribution to the overall success.

This afternoon, focus on the objectives you are working toward and make certain those you are working with also have a clear understanding of the goals that have been set.

Coping Skills

My times are in your hand.
Psalm 31:15 (NRSV)

*H*ow we handle delays tells us a lot about ourselves. How do you handle a traffic jam when you left the house already late for work? What do you do when your flight is delayed because of mechanical difficulty or bad weather? How do you respond when the register in your checkout lane runs out of tape just as you get to the head of the line? Can you take a deep breath and enjoy a five-minute break at the railroad crossing when the guard rail goes down to allow a train to pass?

Consider how one man handled a delay. Just as the light turned green at the busy intersection, his car stalled in heavy traffic. He tried everything he knew to get the car started again, but all his efforts failed. The chorus of honking behind him put him on edge, which only made matters worse.

Finally he got out of his car and walked back to the first driver and said, "I'm sorry, but I can't seem to get my car started. If you'll go up there and give it a try, I'll stay here and blow your horn for you."

Things rarely go as smoothly as we would like, and we don't usually schedule ourselves any extra time "just in case" something goes wrong.

The ability to accept disappointments, delays, and setbacks with a pleasant, generous spirit is a gift of graciousness that comes from one who has received grace from others in pressured circumstances. Life is a series of choices and no matter what situation we are in, we *always* have the freedom to choose how we are going to respond.

Refuse to get out of sorts the next time your schedule gets interrupted or turned upside down. Pray for strength to remain calm, cheerful, relaxed, and refreshed in the midst of the crisis. And always remember: God's plans for you are not thwarted by delays!

Cut Loose!

*Live as free men, yet without using your freedom
as a pretext for evil; but live as servants of God.*
1 Peter 2:16 (RSV)

An old farmer in northern India brought his goods to sell at the village bazaar. Among the items was a whole covey of quail. In order to keep them together, he tied a string around one leg of each bird and attached the strings to a ring which fit over a stick driven into the ground. The farmer exercised the birds by training them to walk around and around in a circle.

For most of the day, the farmer had no offers on the quail. Then along came a devout religious man of the highest Hindu caste. He had great reverence for all of life and felt deep, profound compassion for the little birds walking in a never-ending circle.

The religious man asked the farmer the price of the quail and then offered to buy them all. The farmer was elated. As the holy man handed him the money, however, the farmer was startled to hear him say, "Now, please set them all free."

"What did you say?" the farmer asked.

The holy man repeated himself, saying, "You heard me. Cut the strings from their legs and turn them loose. Set them all free!"

Without another word, the farmer did as he was told. After all, the birds were no longer his — he had been compensated for them. Now what do you think the quail did? They continued their circular march around the center pole. When the religious man attempted to shoo them away, they landed not too far away and resumed their march.[25]

Old habits and thought patterns can keep us from being what God wants us to be and what God wants us to do. To be set free, there are times we must give ourselves a gentle "push," and other times we must receive a "nudge" from someone else. One thing is certain, God desires us to live in freedom — a freedom Jesus purchased for us by way of the cross and resurrection.

We Gather Together

Share with God's people who are in need.
Practice hospitality.
Romans 12:13 (NIV)

One of the greatest pleasures in life is a home-cooked evening meal. What a relief after a hard day to sit down in the late afternoon at a table set with familiar plates and filled with bowls of our favorite foods. What a joy to look up from our places and see the loving faces of family or friends.

During a meal like this we reconnect with those we love, unwind, and speak our minds with no fear of censure. It's a time to be our comfortable selves. For an Amish family in Illinois, however, it also became a way to pay a debt.

Nine-year-old Samuel was in a terrible accident. Mangled by a machine used to grind up corn stalks, he almost lost his arms and legs. It took 28 operations to save his life and three of his limbs. His family was grateful for the medical treatment he received, but daunted by the six-figure bill. The Amish community usually helps itself in these situations, but this was beyond their ability.

The family's solution was to open their home to strangers each weekend. People came for dinner and left a donation at the end of the meal. After five years, about half of the medical bill had been paid.

More important than the money, though, was the emotional impact on the family and their visitors. Those who came to dinner were touched by the simple Amish way of life and the happiness they saw in their hosts. The family was overwhelmed by the number of people who were eager to help, and by the encouraging cards and letters sent to them.

In times of need, we don't always like to ask for help. We prefer to give rather than receive. We wonder what we possibly have to give during a crisis.

An Amish family gave of themselves — their home, their fellowship, and good, nourishing food lovingly prepared. Around a simple table in rural Illinois, family and guests alike received an unforgettable lesson in giving and receiving.

The Plaster Solution

A man hath joy by the answer of his mouth:
and a word spoken in due season, how good is it!
Proverbs 15:23

Disagreements are a natural part of working together— and different points of view are critical to the creative and problem-solving processes. Still, the friction caused when differing opinions arise can cause needless pain and waste valuable time and energy. Occasionally, the best way to convince someone of your point of view while maintaining clear lines of communication is just to keep quiet and start plastering.

Benjamin Franklin learned that plaster sown in the fields would make things grow. He told his neighbors, but they did not believe him, arguing that plaster could be of no use at all to grass or grain.

After a little while he allowed the matter to drop. But he went into the field early the next spring and sowed some grain. Close by the path, where men would walk, he traced some letters with his finger and put plaster into them.

After a week or two the seed sprang up. His neighbors, as they passed that way, gasped at what they saw. Brighter green than all the rest of the field sprouted Franklin's seeded message in large letters, "This has been plastered."

Benjamin Franklin did not need to argue with his neighbors about the benefit of plaster any longer!

The answer to some disagreements may be to stop talking and try out several solutions together, measure them against like standards, and then resume the selection process. Meanwhile, tempers cool, objectivity returns, and new options can surface.

Seventy Times Seven

Forgive, and you will be forgiven.
Luke 6:37 (NKJV)

When one boy hit another during her Sunday school class, a teacher's aid took the offending child outside for discipline. She then assigned a crafts project to the rest of the class so she could talk to the child who had been hit. "You need to forgive Sam for hitting you, Joey," she said.

"Why?" Joey asked. "He's mean. He doesn't deserve any forgiveness."

The teacher said, "The disciples of Jesus may have felt that same way. They asked Jesus how many times they had to forgive someone who was mean to them and Jesus said seventy times seven." (See Matthew 18:22.) Joey sat thoughtfully and the teacher continued, "Do you know how many times that is, Joey?"

Joey had just learned how to multiply, so he took a nearby pencil and piece of paper and worked this math puzzle. Upon getting his answer, he looked up at the teacher and said in shock, "Do you mean to tell me that Sam is going to hit me 489 more times! I'm going to be black and blue for forgiving him all year!"

That's the way many of us may feel — perpetually pummeled by those who continue to hurt or wound us, inadvertently or willfully, day in and day out. Memories also can haunt us, causing unforgiveness to spring up again and again. What are we to do? Forgive! It may take 490 times of saying under our breath or in our hearts, "I forgive you," but forgive we must if we are to be free on the inside.

To forgive does not mean another person's behavior has not hurt us or that they were justified in their actions. A wrong may have been committed. But forgiving means saying, "I choose to let you go. I will not hold the memory of this inside me. I will not seek revenge."

In forgiving some people or memories, we may very well have to "let go" 490 times. But in the end, we will be free, and the other person will be in God's hands.

Tea-Time Manners

The desire of a man is his kindness.
Proverbs 19:22

How much sweeter everyday life would be if tea-time manners were valued. Tea-time manners are more than waving a pinkie in the air, knowing which fork to use, or where to place one's napkin after a meal. These are secondary to the real reason we have manners.

Manners are merely behaving as though Jesus were our honored guest — as if every other person we meet is His personal emissary. It means doing and saying what makes others feel comfortable.

Some years ago, the members of an entire church in Scotland were able to produce one of the most remarkable preachers of the time just by showing him Christlike manners. Here's what happened:

Ian Maclaren, author of Beside the Bonnie Brier Bush, was learning to preach without notes at his first church assignment in the Highlands. At times, he would stop in the middle of a sermon and say to the congregation, "Friends, that is not very clear. It was clear in my study on Saturday, but now I will begin again."

After one particular service when his memory had failed him, Maclaren was approached by a gaunt elder who took him by the hand and said, "When you are not remembering your sermon, just call out a psalm, and we will be singing that while you are taking a rest; for we all are loving you and praying for you."

With such parishioners, how could Ian Maclaren have done anything other than grow in his preaching abilities and pulpit composure? That first Highland church made Ian Maclaren. Years later he said, "I am in the ministry today because of those country folk, those perfect gentlemen and Christians."

If one has developed a sense of manners, then he or she is less likely to have to stop and say, "What would Jesus do in this situation?" Such a person has already been trained to do it.

Pay Attention

Walk in wisdom...redeeming the time.
Colossians 4:5 (NKJV)

A friend of Episcopalian Bishop Phillips Brooks said to him, "I have no time in my life for Christianity. You don't know how hard I work from morning until night. My life is so full, where can I find time for Christianity?"

Brooks responded, "It is as if the engine had said it had no room for the steam. It is as if the tree said it had no room for the sap. It is as if the ocean said it had no room for the tide. It is as if the man had said he had no room for his soul. It is as if the life had said it had no time to live. It is not something added to life; it is life. A man is not alive without it. And for a man to say, 'I am so full in life that I have no room for life,' is an absurdity!"[26]

Our society, like Brooks' friend, is obsessed with time. We try to stay "on schedule" and "be on time."

Pay Attention

On holidays, days off from work, and on vacations, we want to "make the most of time." Our usual lament is that there is just "not enough time."

There are two Greek words for the English word time. *Chronos,* where we get the word chronology, refers to measured time — the time on a clock, the days, weeks, and months of a calendar. *Kairos* time, however, means purposeful time, time which God has filled with meaning, the "right" time.

We have all experienced "kairos" moments — times when everything came together, times when it was "right" to make an important call or write a crucial letter, apply for a particular job, or have a decisive talk with a friend or spouse. These are moments when we gain insight or renewed perspective, see the bigger picture, and discern God's hand is bringing together the fragments of our life.

How do the ticking moments of the clock become filled with a sense of God's time? To turn chronos time into kairos time we need to "take time off" for reflection and quiet. Our resting is not passive inactivity, but an intentional commitment to pay attention to God in all the times of our life.

Step Right Up

Blessed are those who hear the joyful blast of the trumpet,
for they shall walk in the light of your presence.
Psalm 89:15 (TLB)

"Getting away from it all" takes on a whole new meaning when you decide, as a young Scottish girl did, to walk around the world. A troubled home life convinced her she needed a change of scenery, as well as a challenge that would test her mettle.

How does one go about walking around the world? In Ffyona's case, she spent eleven years and covered more than 19,000 miles walking from northern Scotland to southern England; New York to Los Angeles; Sydney to Perth, Australia; and South Africa to Morocco. Along the way, she fought disease, poisonous insects, bad weather, blisters, stonings, and loneliness.

To keep herself going, she had to come up with a way to motivate her often tired feet. She quickly discovered that if she could focus her mind on doing what had to be done to make it through each phase of the walk, her body would do the rest. The stronger her mind, the better her body performed.

Another of Ffyona's important discoveries — to take one day at a time. Each day she would say to herself, "If I walk ten miles right now, I can stop and have a meal." Building in breaks and small rewards along the way made it much easier for her to stay committed to her bigger goal.[27]

Walking seems like such a simple thing to do. But, oh, the power of a walk! Even when we have no particular destination, our feet can take us to a new place and give us both a physical and a psychological break from where we've been. Walking away from a heated debate is sometimes the smartest thing to do and the best way to protect a relationship. Crossing a room to talk to someone who looks lonely is often the first step in building a new friendship.

"The steps of good men are directed by the Lord." (Psalm 37:23 TLB).

Best Friends

You were called into the fellowship
of his Son, Jesus Christ our Lord.
1 Corinthians 1:9 (NRSV)

A student working on her doctoral thesis spent a year on a reservation in the Southwest living with a group of Navajo Indians. As the student did her research she became part of a Native American family. She slept in their home, ate their food, worked with them, and generally lived their lifestyle.

The grandmother in the family did not speak English, yet she and the student were able to form a close bond of friendship. They spent much time together, forging a relationship that was meaningful to each one, yet difficult to explain to anyone else. The two shared experiences together even though they could not talk with each other. In spite of the language difference, they came to a closeness and mutual understanding and affection.

Over the months each one of them worked to learn phrases in the other one's language. The student learned some Navajo phrases and the old grandmother picked up some English words.

When the year ended it was time for the student to return to campus to write her thesis. The tribe held a going-away celebration in honor of her stay and their friendship. The celebration was a sad occasion, because the young woman had become close to the entire village; she would miss them and they would miss her.

As the student climbed into her pickup truck to leave, her dear friend, the old grandmother, came to say good-bye. With tears flowing down her cheeks, the grandmother put her hands on either side of the student's face. She looked directly into the young woman's eyes and said in her newly-learned words: "I like me best when I'm with you."

Good friends are the ones around whom we "like ourselves best" because they have a way of bringing out the best in us. Jesus is that kind of Friend to us. We can share *all* of our life with Him and He still accepts us with His great love. He will bring out the best in us so we can say to Him, "I like me best when I'm with You."

Late-Breaking News

He is the living God, and steadfast forever;
His kingdom is the one which shall not be destroyed,
and His dominion shall endure to the end.
Daniel 6:26 (NKJV)

There's a certain amount of fear that knocks at our hearts when we hear a newscaster say, "This just in...an item of late-breaking news." Most of us would rather not have late-breaking news because, whether of a positive or negative nature, such news interrupts our lives. It upsets our carefully balanced apple cart.

Our spouse calls to say, "I'll be late," when we've made plans for a nice evening together.

We receive word that a loved one is seriously ill just days before our international vacation trip.

We are nearing completion of a major project when our supervisor announces, "I have some impor-tant information that needs to be considered or included in your report."

Late-Breaking News

Such late-breaking news can send us reeling. What we need is a strong dose of adaptability and flexibility, coupled with an extra measure of courage. Author David E. Lilienthal once noted that the genius of America was its ability to make adjustments. "We are adaptable," he wrote, "and because we are adaptable, we are strong."

There is a strength that comes when we allow ourselves to bend without breaking, to adjust without panic, to make midcourse corrections without abandoning the hope of our final destination.

Jesus called His disciples to "follow" Him, but He didn't tell them exactly where He was going or what He would be doing on any given day. Jesus continually adjusted His course to accommodate others in need, and He challenges us to do the same. The good news is that, while circumstances and situations around us may be forever in flux, our relationship with the Lord is sure and fixed. He does not change. He is *always* our Savior, Lord, Teacher, Redeemer, Comforter, Counselor, Rock, and Lover of our Souls!

How important it is that we remember that when late-breaking news comes our way!

Halt!

*Let us strip off anything that slows us down
or holds us back, and especially those sins that
wrap themselves so tightly around our feet and trip us up.*
Hebrews 12:1 (TLB)

Those who counsel the clinically depressed often suggest the HALT! Method to their patients. HALT is an acronym based upon these four words:

- Hungry
- Angry
- Lonely
- Tired

Too much of any of these conditions can result in a stress overload and lead to a downward spiral that eventually crashes into a form of depression. When two or more of these conditions are present, the downward plunge happens faster, with greater pain. And, if all four conditions are present as an ongoing pattern in a person's life, the person's depression may not only be deep, but life itself may be endangered.

To compound the problem, hunger, anger, loneliness, and exhaustion tend to cluster together. If you are overly tired, it's easier to become angry. If you have missed a meal, you are likely to get tired more quickly, and so forth.

Therefore, any time you are feeling too hungry, too angry, too lonely, or too tired...it's time to call a HALT! and to take immediate remedial action. Have a healthy bite to eat. Release your anger in prayer, exercise, or an act of reconciliation. Call a friend and pour out your heart. Take a nap or go to bed early.

"Call it to a halt," and "enough is enough," are well-known phrases we need to apply on a daily basis. Don't neglect your personal nutrition. Get enough sleep. Balance your life with friendships. Live in peace with the people around you.

As you prepare to come to the end of your work day, it's especially important you remember to HALT! Don't push yourself into overdrive, even if you have to work overtime. Avoid setting yourself up for a crash by staying well-fed, calm, in touch with friends, and refreshed.

Sweet Revenge?

*Therefore if thine enemy hunger, feed him; if he thirst, give him
drink: for in so doing thou shalt heap coals of fire on his head.
Be not overcome of evil, but overcome evil with good.*
Romans 12:20-21

A young and hot-tempered officer in the army
struck a foot soldier. The foot soldier was also young, and
noted for his courage. He felt the insult deeply, but
military discipline forbade him to return the blow. He said
with conviction, however, "I will make you repent it."

One day in the heat of battle the foot soldier saw
an officer who was wounded and separated from his
company. He gallantly forced his way through enemy
lines to the officer, whom he recognized as the one who
had insulted him. Nevertheless, he supported the
wounded man with one arm as the two fought their
way back to their own lines.

Trembling with emotion, the officer grasped the
hand of the soldier and stammered out his gratitude,

"Noble man! What a return for an insult so carelessly given!"

The young man pressed his hand in turn, and with a smile said gently, "I told you I would make you repent it." From that time on they were as brothers.

John Wesley found another positive and helpful way to settle quarrels. In his journal he wrote of a disagreement that took place in one of the religious gatherings called Societies. Fourteen people were expelled from the group as a result. Not seeing any good reason why such an action should have taken place, Wesley called the entire group together to try to bring about reconciliation.

Prior to the sermon, prayer, and communion, Wesley recalls, "I willingly received them all again; requiring only one condition of the contenders on both sides, to say not one word of anything that was past." He then goes on to describe the healing that took place in the group when the recounting of old wounds was eliminated as a possibility.

Extending God's grace to those who have wronged us can repair just about any broken relationship. Instead of returning anger with anger, kindness proves the best peacemaker.

Missed Manners

Before honour is humility.
Proverbs 15:33

During the Coolidge Administration, an overnight guest at the White House found himself in a terribly embarrassing predicament. At the family breakfast table he was seated at the President's right hand. To his surprise he saw Coolidge take his coffee cup, pour the greater portion of its contents into the deep saucer, and leisurely add a little bit of cream and sugar.

The guest was so disconcerted he lost his head. With a panicky feeling that it was incumbent upon him to do as the President did, he hastily poured his own coffee into his saucer. But he froze with horror as he watched Coolidge place his own saucer on the floor for the cat![28]

We may never have been guests at the White House, but we have all been in uncomfortable situations where we were unsure of ourselves and the proper etiquette for the occasion. Scripture describes the proper protocol for entering the presence of God. The psalmist tells us, "Enter into His gates with thanksgiving, and into His courts with praise" (Psalm 100:4 NKJV). We go into the Lord's presence with gratitude and joy for all He is and does in our lives.

King David asked, "Who may ascend into the hill of the Lord? Or who may stand in His holy place?" and then answered, "He who has clean hands and a pure heart, who has not lifted up his soul to an idol, nor sworn deceitfully" (Psalm 24:3-4 NKJV).

The writer of the Book of Hebrews said that Jesus made a way to God for us. We can approach His throne with confidence and "receive mercy and find grace to help us in our time of need" (Hebrews 4:16 NIV).

We don't have to worry about *how* we come to the Lord when we approach with pure and expectant hearts, understanding that before honor comes humility.

Planting and Reaping

Sow for yourselves righteousness; reap in mercy;
break up your fallow ground, for it is time to seek the Lord,
till He comes and rains righteousness on you.
Hosea 10:12 (NKJV)

Have you ever come out of the grocery store or flower shop and said to yourself, "Someday I'm going to grow my own vegetables and flowers"? Perhaps it was price, quality, or the frustration of standing in line to pay that gave you this urge.

Then "someday" finally came, and you found yourself on your hands and knees in the back yard — digging, fertilizing, planting, watering, pruning, and weeding. A small piece of land became a much-loved, well-tended oasis.

Have you noticed what happens when you garden? Yes, the joints ache, fingernails break, sweat rolls off of you, and your hands and clothes get full of dirt. But something happens to your spirit as well.

Planting and Reaping

A couple with five children were very wise in the raising of their family. They decided to plant a vegetable garden. The children thought its sole purpose was to keep enough food on the table, but their parents had something else in mind. When a child was fretting over some problem or not getting along with the others, Mom or Dad would send them to the garden for a weeding break. By the time one of the parents arrived to check on their progress, the troubled child was ready to talk or had worked out his aggressions.

Taking a break each day to till the soil helps us regain our equilibrium. By putting us in contact with some of the basic elements of existence — sun, air, water, soil — it removes us totally from whatever it is we normally do to maintain our lives.

A pursuit like gardening teaches us patience, redefines our definition of beauty, and gives us confidence in our ability to do something constructive. As we learn to care for something besides ourselves, we have more to give to others when we put aside our hoes and trowels and return to our "other" world.

One of the best places to go after a hard day of work is home...to the garden!

Tea Time with God

Count On It!

Jesus Christ is the same yesterday and today and for ever.
Hebrews 13:8 (RSV)

Tea is the second-largest consumer beverage in the world — ranking only behind water. Its origins reach back four thousand years in time. The story goes that one day the Chinese Emperor Shen Nung knelt before a fire while he was boiling water. The wise Emperor was called the "Divine Healer," and always boiled water before drinking it. Nobody knew the causes of illnesses, but Shen Nung had observed that people who boiled their drinking water had better health.

Shen Nung's servants had made a fire from the branch of a nearby tree. As the water began to boil, some of the topmost leaves of the branches were blown into the pot of water.

The Emperor exclaimed, "What a delightful aroma!" as the fragrance of tea floated into the air for the first time. He then sipped the aromatic steaming liquid. "Ah!" he said, "What a flavor!" And that is how tea was discovered in China in the year 2737 B.C. Tea is now consumed in every nation of the world.[29]

Society today places great value on *newness*. Seminars, workshops, and conferences abound, each offering new methods and formulas to achieve success. Stores advertise new styles of shoes, clothing, wallpaper, furniture, and electronics. If it's new, it's good!

But is newness always the best?

Two thousand years ago Jesus said, "I am the way, the truth and the life" (John 14:6 NKJV) and His Word is true today. You can count on it, no matter what new ideas you encounter in the world. As you sip your tea — just as people have for centuries — remind yourself that God's Word stands the test of time and serves as your foundation in every situation.

A Heart for Art

Do good, O Lord, to those who are good,
and to those who are upright in their hearts.
Psalm 125:4 (NASB)

Whether you prefer coffee or tea, there's something special about going to a coffee house or tearoom — places specifically created for sitting down with a warm mug and basking in a soothing ambiance. And if you happen to find yourself at Cafe Lam in Hanoi some afternoon, you can also enjoy gazing at a small portion of the owner's priceless art collection.

Nguyen Van Lam began selling coffee from a cart in 1950. Several years later, he bought a building near an art school. Many of his customers were struggling art students who could barely afford to put food in their stomachs, much less buy art supplies. Lam, an impassioned art lover, loaned them money so they could practice their craft.

Several of the artists — who later became quite famous — repaid Lam's generosity with paintings, prints, and drawings. Over the years, Lam's collection grew to more than a thousand pieces of art. Only a small portion of the collection is displayed in the cafe, but it covers almost every square inch of wall space.

Lam's extensive collection is a precious treasure. To protect the art during the war, Lam even went to the extent of storing the art in an air-raid shelter. These days, he hopes to turn his building into a museum to permanently display his collection for future generations to enjoy.

Lam loves artists as much as he loves art. He admires their generous spirits, their ability to find beauty in everything, and the way they pour themselves into their work without demanding something back.

To casual passersby, the building that houses Cafe Lam is a dilapidated, nothing-to-look-at edifice. But for those willing to come inside, there is a cup of good coffee, and beauty as far as the eye can see.[30]

Time with Jesus can be time spent in a lovely art gallery, where He shows you all the colors and patterns of your life. Just as Lam cared for the struggling artists, Jesus cares for you. He is your comforter, friend, protector, and the source of all creativity and beauty. Thank Him today for His love for you.

Redirected Anger

A gentle answer turns away wrath,
but a harsh word stirs up anger.
Proverbs 15:1 (NIV)

A Salvation Army officer stationed in New Zealand tells of an old Maori woman who won the name Warrior Brown for her fighting ability when she was drunk or enraged. After her conversion to Christianity, she was asked to give her testimony at an open-air meeting. One of her old enemies took the opportunity to loudly make fun of her. He ended his harangue by throwing a large potato at her, which hit her with a nasty blow.

The crowd grew deadly silent. A week earlier, the cowardly insulter would have needed to sprint into hiding to salvage his teeth. But what a different response they witnessed that night!

Warrior picked up the potato without a word and put it in her pocket. No more was heard of the incident until the harvest festival came around, when she appeared with a little sack of potatoes to share. She explained she had cut up and planted the potato and was now presenting it to the Lord as part of her increase.

Warrior had learned how to live in peace with her neighbors and yet be a strong spiritual "warrior" for the Lord's cause. What a beautiful example of taking the ill men do and turning it into praise for the Father in heaven!

President Lincoln was once taken to task for his amiable attitude toward his enemies. "Why do you try to make friends of them?" asked an associate. "You are a powerful man. You should try to destroy them."

"Am I not destroying my enemies," Lincoln gently replied, "when I make them my friends?"

What might you do today to show kindness to an enemy? When you treat your enemy as a friend, and your enemy responds in friendship, you have turned your enemy into your friend!

Open the Door

Behold, I stand at the door, and knock: if any man
hear my voice, and open the door, I will come in
to him, and will sup with him, and he with me.
Revelation 3:20

A nurse on duty in a pediatric ward often gave the children an opportunity to listen to their own hearts with her stethoscope. One day she put the stethoscope into a little boy's ears. She asked him, "Can you hear that? What do you suppose that is?"

The little boy frowned a moment, caught up in the wonder of this strange tapping inside his chest. Then he broke into a grin and responded, "Is that Jesus knocking?"

Another story is told of a group of students who went to visit a great religious teacher. The wise teacher asked the young scholars a seemingly obvious question. "Where is the dwelling place of God?"

The students laughed among themselves and replied, "What a thing to ask! Is not the whole world full of His glory?"

The learned old man smiled and replied, "God dwells wherever man lets him in."

The little boy listening to his heart through the stethoscope seemed to have more wisdom than the group of students. With his innocent, trusting faith, he had no problem believing that Jesus was knocking on his heart's door.

Imagine your life to be a house of many rooms. Each room represents a different aspect of your life. Some of the rooms are messed up, others are clean and tidy. The doors that are locked represent areas where you have not invited Jesus to enter.

Like the little boy, when we hear Jesus knocking at the closed doors of our life, it is up to us to open the door and let Him in. Even those rooms that are dark and frightening are filled with light and understanding when Jesus enters.

Downshifting

He who dwells in the shelter of the Most High
will rest in the shadow of the Almighty.
Psalm 91:1 (NIV)

A few years ago, an automobile manufacturer used the slogan, "We are driven." The auto maker might have been talking about most of the human race! We are a people on a mission: work nonstop, master the learning curve, achieve as much as possible as fast as we can.

For all our enthusiasm and energy, however, we start out strong in the morning and then fall prey to gloomy weather, dark moods, or weariness toward tea time. We feel driven to finish what's in front of us, but we don't have the stamina to go on. That's when we have to resort to Plan B.

Plan B says that if you don't want to leave your office yet, but you are burned out on weightier matters, you have to do something lighter. Select a job-related task that doesn't require a lot of brain power.

Write a letter, organize a file, type some notes, gather reference materials, return a phone call, or write memory-joggers on your calendar for up-coming meetings. Give your eyes a break from the computer screen and close them for a couple of minutes. (When the eyes are closed for at least 30 seconds, a natural lubrication takes place, making eyes feel more refreshed.)

"When it is dull and cold and weary weather with us, when the light is hidden, and the mists are thick, and the sleet begins to fall, still we may get on with the work which can be done as well in the dark days as in the bright; work which otherwise will have to be hurried through in the sunshine, taking up its happiest and most fruitful hours," said Bishop Francis Paget in *The Spirit of Discipline*. "Very often, I think, the plainer work is the best way of getting back into the light and warmth....Through humbly and simply doing what we can, we retrieve the power of doing what we would."

Until your concentration level is back to normal, switch to automatic pilot and glide for a little while!

His Way

In quietness and in confidence shall be your strength.
Isaiah 30:15

A Danish author tells the story of an old peasant who made an unusual request of his son as he lay dying. He asked his son to go into the best room of the house every day and sit there alone for half an hour. The son agreed to the strange request and promised his father he would do what he had been asked.

After his father's death, the son kept faithful to his promise. He did this unusual thing — spending a half hour alone each day. At first the time of quiet and solitude was uncomfortable. He became restless and anxious for the time to end. But over the weeks, that half hour of solitude grew into a cherished and even transforming habit. The son looked forward to this brief quiet period each day and even began to thrive on it. He began to experience deep and calming changes within himself.[31]

Are you willing to be alone for fifteen or thirty minutes each day, preferably when your mind is not overtired? Are you willing to take an adventure of expectant faith, not looking for a predefined experience, not seeking an emotional high, but asking Jesus to come to you in His own way?

With your body relaxed and comfortable, and looking only to Jesus, your heart will be turned to Him in adoration. From this experience, you are likely to have a greater desire to obey Him. People who devote time to be alone with the Lord find a renewed reservoir of personal strength and quiet confidence.

The world desperately needs people who are trying out Jesus' way of life and have an ever-deepening experience of Him. They are looking for peace and joy that lasts, and those qualities only show up in the lives of believers who allow Jesus to reign in their hearts.

Spend some peaceful moments alone with the Lord today and watch the peace and joy in your heart grow and spill over into the lives of others.

Loosen Your Ties

*Trust in the Lord with all your heart, and lean
not on your own understanding; in all your ways
acknowledge Him, and He shall direct your paths.*
Proverbs 3:5-6 (NKJV)

"*L*oosen your tie" are three of the sweetest words
you can ever speak to a man who has had a harried
business day and is eager to relax.

In a broader more figurative sense, we all can
benefit from "loosening our ties" occasionally. This
does not mean we need to let go of relationships,
ideals, or concerns that are important to us. However,
it does mean there are times when we need to hold
relationships and projects a little less tightly.

- Be less concerned with who gets the credit.
- Be less uptight that some things may not be
  done to perfection. In most cases, our best effort
  is not only acceptable, but allows others to be
  more comfortable.

- Trust others to make their own decisions and choices.

- Allow others an opportunity to participate, rather than feel you need to do it all or be responsible for everything.

- Give others the freedom to make mistakes and learn from them.

- Give others room to breathe, to grow, to expand, and to have a little fun.

We need to loosen the ties of total control. We need to relinquish our hold and turn the reins over to the Lord, trusting Him to bring to pass His perfect will and His ultimate purpose in our lives.

Most of us wouldn't have trusted Jesus' group of twelve disciples, especially Peter who denied Him, to carry on the leadership of the Church, but Jesus did. If He can trust us to do His work on this earth — something which impacts eternity — surely we can trust others a little more with our important tasks and projects.

Loosen your grip on everything except Jesus!

An Open Door

I run in the path of your commands,
for you have set my heart free.
Psalm 119:32 (NIV)

One warm summer afternoon, a woman was attending the baptism of her grandniece in a great old stone church in the English countryside. The massive doors of the church were flung wide to allow the warm sunshine into the chilly stone structure.

As she sat enjoying the ritual, a small bird flew in through the open doors. Full of fear, it flew backward and forward near the ceiling, vainly looking for a way out into the sunshine. Seeing the light coming through the dark stained glass windows, it flew to one, then the next, and finally back toward the ceiling. It continued flying about in this way for several minutes, quickly exhausting its strength in frenzied panic. The woman watched the bird with concern and frustration. How foolish he was not to fly back out the same door through which he had entered!

Nearly ready to fall to the floor, the bird made a final lunge for one of the large rafters. Realizing he was in no immediate danger, he hopped a little on the beam, turned around, and suddenly saw the open door. Without hesitation he flew out into the sunshine, loudly singing a joyful song as he went.

The bird had captivated the woman's imagination. Suddenly she realized that she was like the bird. She had flitted about, trying to live a "good" life of noble works without recognizing that the door of salvation had been open to her all the time. She suddenly understood that to avoid flying errantly into places that offered no hope of eternal life, she need only stop flapping and be still in the Lord's presence. From that vantage point, she could better see the door of grace that He had prepared for her.

During your tea time break today, let your spirit fly up to a high place and sit with the Lord. He will show you how to fly out of your current problems.

The "Off" Switch

The Lord is my shepherd,...He leads me beside
quiet waters. He restores my soul.
Psalm 23:1-3 (NASB)

When you were a child, how many times did you hear a parent say, "Turn off the light when you leave the room!" Sometimes a brief lecture about the high cost of electricity or the importance of being good stewards of the world's energy resources followed.

There comes a point in each work day when we need to turn off the lights by closing our eyes or dimming the light. At the same time, we need to...turn off the noise! Turn off the beeper. Unplug the phone. Shut down the computer. Turn off the television set, radio, or stereo. Close the door and turn off the sounds of the hallway, the city, the commotion in the next room.

Those who lived through the air raids of World War II have remarked with great consistency that the best sound in the world to them was the sound of silence — no sirens blaring in the night, no bombs bursting, no airplanes droning overhead, no sounds of families scurrying to shelters. Silence was precious beyond words. It meant life.

Our senses are bombarded by more visual, auditory, and olfactory sensations than at any time in history. At times we need to give ourselves rest and turn off the lights and sounds around us...even if we don't leave the room! It is then that we can hear in our hearts what is truly important.

The prophet Elijah knew firsthand the truth of this. While hiding out in a remote cave, he was directed by the Lord to stand on the mountain as He passed by. Elijah first experienced a mighty wind...and then an earthquake...and then a raging fire...and then the sound of a "still, small voice." Elijah went out and stood in the entrance to the cave, for he knew that this was the voice of God. (See 1 Kings 19:12.)

Be still and be a good steward of your resources. Allow yourself to enjoy a time of solitude and silence. Let the Lord restore your soul.

Tools of the Trade

We are his workmanship.
Ephesians 2:10 (RSV)

*W*e see it as we walk along an ocean shore, where steep cliffs meet with the rise and fall of the tides. The splashing of sand- and rock-laden waves have cut away at the towering sea cliffs. Day after day, night after night, the continual lapping of the ocean water silently undercuts the stone walls. Then in one sudden blow the entire structure can shift and fall thundering into the sea. On a daily basis, the wear and tear of water on sea cliffs is imperceptible, yet we know that every wave hitting the rock is washing away some of its hard surface.

We see the same shaping influence in another aspect of nature — trees that grow at the timberline, a harsh, remote setting. The extra resins that flow in the trees, as a result of the severe winds and snowstorms at the timberline, produce a grain of wood that has a rare and desirable texture.

Such wood is sought by violin makers because it produces instruments of the finest quality and resonance. Fierce storms, the short growing season, and whipping winds combine to yield some of the choicest wood in all the world.[32]

Every person subjected to the endless wear and tear of life develops faults and cracks in their life. In God's hands, however, those stresses and changes become His tools for shaping our life for His purpose. As our lives are yielded to and shaped by Him, He creates within us the ability to resonate His presence.

The varied and often difficult experiences of life, given to God, are how He transforms each individual into something beautiful. The Holy Spirit can work wonders on the rough edges of our stubborn wills and hard hearts, conforming them to His own will.

Commit your life to the Lord again this afternoon. Trust Him to take all that happens to you — both good and bad — and make you stronger and wiser, using you in His great plan.

Lightening Up

*Blessed be the Lord, for He has made marvelous His
lovingkindness to me in a besieged city.*
Psalm 31:21 (NASB)

Are you a strict constructionist or a loose
constructionist? These terms came into vogue after the
U.S. Constitution was adopted. A strict constructionist
takes the document exactly as it is; a loose constructionist
sees room for different applications and interpretations.

When it comes to your daily schedule, are you
strict or loose? Do you refuse to deviate from your To-
Do List, or are you easygoing enough to shift gears
when opportunity knocks at your door?

A young mother with four small children had
given up on ever finding time for a break. Her husband
frequently worked overtime, which meant she was
totally responsible for taking care of the house and the
children. She had decided the only way to make it all
work was to be as rigid as a drill sergeant.

Certain chores had to be performed at a set time each day and on certain days of the week. If not, she felt pressured to make up for lost time by staying up later or getting up earlier...which drained her energy, made her cranky, and resulted in getting less done the following day.

One afternoon, her five-year-old daughter came into the kitchen, where she was planning dinner. "Come to my tea party," she said, a big smile on her face. Normally, Mom would have said, "Not now; I'm busy." But that day she had a flashback to her own five-year-old self inviting her mother to a tea party and being turned down.

Instead of saying no, she helped her daughter put together a tray containing a plate of cookies, some sandwiches cut into bite-size pieces, a small pot of tea, sugar and cream, her best teaspoons, and a couple of linen napkins. The two oldest children were at school. The youngest was napping. The house was quiet, and the young mother couldn't remember when she'd enjoyed a cup of tea so much.

Grace

*And the child grew, and waxed strong in spirit, filled with
wisdom: and the grace of God was upon him.*
Luke 2:40

The very act of serving tea brings to mind the
word "grace." Traditionally, afternoon tea is a graceful
act in the weariest part of the day. A beautiful way to
enjoy tea time is to use it as a special celebration of the
grace of our Lord. Take a few moments to sing His
praise or to read aloud lyrics that exalt His presence in
our lives. One hymn you might consider singing is this
one by J. E. Myhill:

He Giveth More Grace
He giveth more grace when the burdens grow greater.
He sendeth more strength when the labor's increase.
To added affliction He addeth His mercy,
To multiplied trials, His multiplied peace.

When we have exhausted our store of endurance,
When our strength has failed ere the day is half done,

When we reach the end of our hoarded resources,
Our Father's full giving has only begun.

His love has no limits, His grace has no measure,
His power no boundary known unto men.
For out of His infinite riches in Jesus,
He giveth, and giveth, and giveth again.[33]

The Lord's grace is beyond measure! We can never consume it all.

Do Be Do Be Do

The Lord looks on the heart.
1 Samuel 16:7 (NRSV)

A father tells of his young daughter who, like many American girls, had a large collection of dolls. Modern dolls, he noted, are far different from their predecessors. Today a girl has a choice of owning a doll that can "walk and talk, drink and wink, slurp, burp, cry, sigh and laugh" — almost anything a real baby does, including wet itself and even get diaper rash.

After years of buying the most modern dolls for his daughter, the man wondered which of these marvels was her favorite. To his surprise, he found she especially liked the small rag doll she had been given on her third birthday.

The novelty of all the other performing dolls had long worn off, but this simple rag doll had allowed her to love it. The other dolls had caught her eye, but the rag doll had won her heart.

Do Be Do Be Do

To his little girl, the rag doll was real and was loved just the way it was — missing both eyes and most of its hair. After all the years and lost parts, the doll was still what it had always been, *just itself*.

Too often, we are like the high-tech dolls. We try to impress others with our skills, talent, education, speech, or other abilities, when what we need to be is simply a person who is willing to be themselves.

Within every person lies the innate desire to be loved, accepted, and pleasing to others. But if we spend all our energy trying to be something we are not, we will never know the joy of being loved for who we are.

Be yourself! Genuine love is not a reward for performance or achievement. People may like or admire you for what you can do, but they will love you for who you are.

Likewise, try to see past others' performances or efforts to gain attention or approval. Try to look past exteriors and outer appearances that may betray the true condition of the heart. Love others for who they are.

"*We interrupt your life . . .*"

I will sing to the Lord all my life;
I will sing praise to my God as long as I live.
Psalm 104:33 (NIV)

Living longer is supposed to be a good thing. None of us wants to die "before our time." We want to see children and grandchildren and sometimes great-grandchildren grow up. We want to travel, enjoy the homes we worked so hard to build, and do all those things we dreamed of before and after retirement.

Life doesn't always turn out the way we planned. Yes, we might be living longer, but so are our parents. And oftentimes, parents have major health concerns that require constant care.

As children we were the cared for, but somehow we have become the caregivers. We had our life compartmentalized, but the model has to be broken because Mom or Dad has doctor appointments, therapy sessions, or activities to attend at a senior center — and we are the chauffeurs.

Mom needs groceries and someone to cook her meals. Dad's house needs to be cleaned and the lawn needs mowing. Mom is lonely and needs someone to sit and talk to her for a couple of hours. Dad needs help buying clothes. An adult child's life can disappear in the process of caregiving.

Take positive steps if you find yourself in the role of caregiver for elderly parents. It helps to have a friend you can visit with from time to time — someone who isn't too close to the situation. You need the perspective he or she can give. It also helps to find a support group of people who have learned how to care for their parents with wisdom and joy.

Start each day by saying, "I'll do my best today," and avoid criticizing yourself for not doing everything perfectly. Take care of yourself! You can't help anyone if you get sick due to lack of rest, poor nutrition, or stress.

Above all, make your caregiving an act of love and not obligation. Ask the Lord for His grace and His peace to surround you, whispering prayers to Him throughout the day.

Power Naps

*With him is an arm of flesh; but with us
is the Lord our God to help us, and to fight
our battles. And the people rested themselves
upon the words of Hezekiah king of Judah.*

2 Chronicles 32:8

Have you ever considered trading in your afternoon break for a quick nap?

Medical students are usually adept at taking power naps. They fall asleep immediately upon lying down, sleep for fifteen to twenty minutes, and then awake refreshed. Researchers have discovered these short naps are actually more beneficial than longer midday naps. The body relaxes, but does not fall into a "deep sleep," which can cause grogginess and disorientation.

Only one thing is required for people to sleep this quickly and benefit fully from a power nap — the ability to "turn off the mind." We quiet our minds by not thinking about all that remains to be done, worrying about all that might happen, or fretting over events in the past.

Power nappers are experts at inducing a form of inner peace that comes from knowing all will be well with the world while they check out for a few minutes. What they believe with their minds actually helps their bodies relax.

When King Hezekiah told the people the Lord was with them and would fight their battles, they *rested* upon his words. His words gave them inner peace, confidence, and a rest for their souls. We can take those same words to heart today.

The Lord is with us also, to help us and to fight our battles. These simple lyrics from a Bible-school chorus say it well:

You worry and you wonder how you're gonna get it
done,
from the rising of the moon 'til the setting of the sun.
Plenty to do when your rest is through,
Let Him have the world for a turn or two.

There will be plenty to do when you wake up...so sleep on for a few minutes.

Somebody To Divide With

*But my God shall supply all your need
according to his riches in glory by Christ Jesus.*
Philippians 4:19

At the turn of the century, a man wrote in his diary the story of a young newsboy he met on a street near his home in London. It was well known in the neighborhood that the boy was an orphan. His father had abandoned the family when the boy was a baby, and his mother had died shortly after he began selling newspapers.

All attempts to place the boy in either an institution or a foster home were thwarted, because the boy refused each offer of help and ran away when attempts were made to confine him. "I can take care o' myself jest fine, thank ye!" he would say to kindly old ladies who questioned whether he'd had his porridge that day.

Indeed, he never looked hungry and his persistence at selling papers, load after load, gave the impression he spoke the truth.

Somebody To Divide With

But the streets are a lonely place for a child to live, and the man's diary reflects a conversation he had with the child about his living arrangements. As he stopped to buy his paper one day, the man bought a little extra time by fishing around in his pocket for coins and asked the boy where he lived. He replied that he lived in a little cabin in an impoverished district of the city near the river bank. This was something of a surprise to the man.

With more interest, he inquired, "Well, who lives with you?"

The boy answered, "Only Jim. Jim is crippled and can't do no work. He's my pal."

Now clearly astounded that the child appeared to be supporting not only himself but also someone who was unable to contribute any income, the man noted, "You'd be better off without Jim, wouldn't you?"

The answer came with not a little scorn — a sermon in a nutshell: "No, sir, I couldn't spare Jim. I wouldn't have nobody to go home to. An' say, Mister, I wouldn't want to live and work with nobody to divide with, would you?"

Thirst-Quenchers

Whosoever will, let him take the water of life freely.
Revelation 22:17

*W*ater is essential to the survival of plants, animals, and people. The life processes of an organism depend on its cells having moisture. A tree, for example, may be 80 percent sap, which is primarily water. Sap contains minerals, carbohydrates, vitamins, and proteins, which circulate through the tree's vascular system to feed all parts of the tree.

The amount of the water supply in an area determines whether it is a desert or a forest. It determines whether a tree is shriveled and stunted or towering and majestic. Water comes to trees through dew, clouds, mists, fog, summer rains, and winter snows. Trees also take in water through their roots, which tap into springs, streams, or rivers.

A tree does not hoard moisture for itself, but after the water travels through the framework of the tree, it is given off into the surrounding air. The moisture, along with the oxygen expelled into the air, gives the forest a fresh fragrance.

The spiritual lesson we learn from nature is that it is nearly impossible to be a blessing to others when we are grossly undernourished ourselves. Like the tree, we must be well-watered with God's Word and His Spirit to bring a sweet fragrance to those around us.

If you are feeling empty and dry this afternoon, go to the watering hole of God's Word and take a long, refreshing drink. Feel His truth permeate every cell of your being and rejuvenate love, peace, and joy in your heart. It won't be long until you're looking for ways to help someone else!

Decision-Free Hours

Sing to Him, sing psalms to Him;
talk of His wondrous works!
Glory in His holy name.
Psalm 105:2-3 (NKJV)

Kate declared the hour between three and four o'clock in the afternoon a decision-free hour in her office! She announced this to her staff in a lighthearted way, but was secretly intent upon making this a reality.

As the supervisor of nearly 30 people, all of whom had access to her because of her open-door policy and easy style of management, Kate was asked to make decisions incessantly. This left little time for creative interaction or easy conversation with her staff members and colleagues.

At first, Kate's staff found the habit hard to break. "What can we say if we aren't asking you a question?" her secretary finally asked in a tentative voice.

Decision-Free Hours

❀ · ❀ · ❀ · ❀ · ❀ · ❀ · ❀ · ❀ · ❀ · ❀ · ❀ · ❀ · ❀

"Tell me something!" Kate suggested. "Anything! Tell me something funny that has happened in the office today, or something that is happening in the lives of the staff or their family members. Clue me in to a new idea or give me a creative suggestion. Just don't ask me to make a decision or to respond in any way except to ask a question of my own or make a casual comment."

Over time, Kate found that people were quick to stop by her office between three and four o'clock just to say "hi," to share a bit of news, or to compliment a fellow employee. Her decision-free hour became the most positive hour in the day, and the information she received actually helped her become a better manager — and make wiser decisions.

Could it be that the Lord might also enjoy some decision-free, problem-free, no-answer-required-from-Me hours with us, His children and coworkers in the world? Could it be that He'd enjoy hearing prayers in which we simply tell Him what is happening, what we find funny or interesting about our lives, and what delights us or gives us joy? Could it be that He'd enjoy hearing a good joke from our lips, rather than a string of incessant petitions?

It just might be.

The Gentle Spirit

But the fruit of the Spirit is love, joy, peace,
longsuffering, gentleness, goodness, faith.
Galatians 5:22

The gentle person is one who knows how to create an atmosphere of acceptance, warmth, and enjoyment for those around him or her. We sometimes hear Jesus called "Gentle Savior" because of His all-loving care and attention. One who imitates His gentleness will always put the feelings of others above his own. An artist named Turner was such a man.

Turner's works were treasured for their bright, intense colors which were blended and juxtaposed with such genius that they nearly extinguished all interest in the paler, subtler hues of paintings that may have been hung near his.

Once his great picture of Cologne, exhibited in 1826, happened to be hung between two portraits by another famous artist, Sir Thomas Lawrence. Sir

Thomas noticed the injurious effect Turner's bright skies had on his portraits. He was troubled and mortified at the possible damage to his reputation. He begged the gallery board to move his paintings, but the position of all the works was set and could not be changed.

Only one option remained. At the time, artists were allowed to retouch their pictures right on the wall of the Academy, and Turner retouched his in such a way that Sir Thomas no longer worried his work might suffer in comparison.

At the exhibition's opening, a friend of Turner's proudly led a group of friends to the painting he had viewed earlier in Turner's studio. He gasped in amazement. The once glorious skies were now dull gray — the picture was ruined. Spying Turner, he ran to him and asked what had happened to his masterpiece.

"Hush!" whispered Turner, "It's nothing. It will all wash off — it's nothing but lampblack. I couldn't bear to see poor Lawrence so unhappy!"

Invisible Work

Faith is the assurance of things hoped for,
the conviction of things not seen.
Hebrews 11:1 (NRSV)

Trees have specific seasons for dormancy — a time when the tree appears to be inactive and not growing. This season of rest comes immediately prior to a season of rapid and accelerated growth. During dormancy, the cells and tissues within the tree are being repaired and built up. This activity is invisible to the eye. The tree is quietly preparing for the vigor of spring.

Dormancy is one of the most important periods in the life cycle of the tree. It is how a tree becomes fit for the later demands of adding new wood to its structure and bearing its fruit.

The benefits of dormancy apply to people as well. There is a mistaken notion that to be effective we must always be active. But people also have seasons in their lives when God is preparing them for what lies ahead.

Not knowing the future ourselves, we often have to come to a deep trust in God during times when nothing seems to be happening in our lives. Inactivity must not be equated with nonproductivity — God is at work behind the scenes!

It takes patience and humility to get through a time of dormancy. Most of us desire to be productive at all times so we can "get ahead" in our lives. We need to recognize there are times when, unbeknownst to us, God has to work in our hearts to prepare us for our destiny.

We need to humble ourselves before Him and realize we didn't create ourselves. We can't know fully what it is we will need in our future. Dormant times call for us to wait on the Lord and trust Him to do His work in our hearts. We can rest assured He is preparing us for something great, in His timing and according to His purpose.

Write Away

And the Lord answered me, and said, Write the vision, and
make it plain upon tables, that he may run that readeth it.
Habakkuk 2:2

As teenagers, our diaries were sacred. Woe to the curious sibling or friend who dared to unlock the secrets of our lives!

Through the centuries, journals have been a precious possession to many, a place to chronicle days, record feelings, dream, complain, plot a course, and escape. Many journals have become valuable historical records, while others have served as the basis for novels or scholarly papers.

Most of us will never see our journals in print — we hope! — but we can benefit greatly from the writing process. Journaling is taking a journey — through the past, the present, or the future.

Some people journal early in the morning, before the day begins, and record dreams from the night before or thoughts about the day ahead. Others journal at night, just before bed, to put the final punctuation on the day. Still others use journaling as a good excuse to take a break during the day.

One woman retreats to a favorite room late in the afternoon, before the family troops in and preparations for the evening meal begin. She sits in a comfortable chair, puts her feet up, sips a cup of tea, listens to some quiet music, and jots down thoughts in her journal. Perhaps she hasn't the chance to do it every day, but she makes the effort to allow at least a few minutes for this stop-the-world-and-let-me-get-off indulgence.

Journaling on paper might not be suited to you. Sitting quietly and thinking about what's happened that day, and then mentally turning the frustrating parts over to God, might be your way of bringing closure to what is beyond your control. However you choose to journal, make and keep a daily appointment with the Lord for reflection. Such a time can help you unjumble your thoughts and find a suitable stride for finishing out your day.

Parsley

But ye are washed, but ye are sanctified
but ye are justified in the name of the Lord Jesus,
and by the Spirit of our God.
1 Corinthians 6:11

Most of us are very familiar with parsley, those sprigs of greenery that give color to our dinner plates in restaurants. Parsley is sometimes used as a lush bedding for salad bars, or as a garnish on pasta dishes and bowls of soup.

For the most part, parsley seems decorative — a pretty splash of green to brighten the culinary scene. Few of us ever eat the parsley made available to us, or even think to try it. And yet that is why parsley was originally provided. It was intended to be eaten in small quantities — a few leaves consumed as the final bite from the plate. For what purpose?

Parsley is a food known to gourmets as a "palate cleanser." Eating it removes the lingering taste of foods just eaten to allow a person to experience more fully the new tastes of the next course. Parsley erases the old and makes way for the new! In fact, after a bite of parsley, most people find it difficult even to recall vividly the flavor of the foods previously eaten.

Another interesting fact about parsley is, if you look closely at a clump of it, you will make an amazing discovery. Like clover, parsley is a "trinity" plant. Each time a stem divides into stalks or leaves, it divides into three parts.

What a wonderful spiritual analogy we have in parsley! For surely it is our Father, Son, and Holy Spirit who cleanse us from the dust, dirt, and evil grime of the world, and prepare us for the beautiful new world which Jesus called the Kingdom of Heaven. God is the one who has the capacity to remove all memories of sorrow and pain and replace them with overflowing joy and hope for the future!

Take another look at your world today. What other lessons does the Lord have for you to learn about His creative wonders? You can be assured — His entire creation points toward Him and to the glorious plan He has for you as His child.

A Servant's Heart

Serve one another in love.
Galatians 5:13 (NIV)

Work is over and you're headed home, but first there are several errands to run. When the last stop has been made and you're pulling into your driveway, you marvel once again at the all-too-common coldness of your fellow humans.

Doesn't anyone smile anymore? Can't people help me find what I'm looking for without treating me like a nuisance? Doesn't anyone apologize for making a person wait or for giving bad service?

The boss of a moving company in the Northeast has a philosophy we wish every person who serves us would emulate. Knowing what a traumatic experience it is to pack up and start a new life in a new place, he makes a point of letting his clients know he understands and cares about what they're going through. In the process, he has found it is just as easy to be kind as it is to be abrupt.

The best example we have of how to serve is the Lord Jesus. In Matthew 20:28 (NIV), He told His disciples, "The Son of Man did not come to be served, but to serve." Jesus' dedication to service was evident in all He did, from teaching in the synagogues and preaching the good news, to healing the sick and performing miracles.

"When he saw the crowds," says Matthew 9:36 (NIV), "he had compassion on them, because they were harassed and helpless, like sheep without a shepherd."

Isn't that the way we sometimes feel at the end of a long, hard day — harassed and helpless? Don't we want someone to treat us kindly and lead us home? When people treat us well — what a difference it makes!

The law of sowing and reaping tells us that what we sow we will reap. (See Galatians 6:7.) As we become more and more a servant of love and kindness to others, we will find ourselves being served with love and kindness.

Fairie Penguins

Behold, how good and how pleasant it is
for brethren to dwell together in unity!
Psalm 133:1

One of the most interesting of all natural
phenomena to witness is the nightly return of the
"fairie penguins" to their rooks in the sand dunes off
southern Australia.

These penguins, only about a foot in height, swim for
days, even weeks, fishing for food. When dusk
approaches, one or more groups of fairie penguins return
home. As if the waves are spurting ink onto the sand,
they spill out of the surf, then gather together in tight
clusters as if gathering the courage to cross the naked
sands. They make a bold dash for the dunes, hopping up
and over any obstacles they encounter, each penguin
hobbling toward its rook on a well-worn, tiny path.

Once at home, each penguin greets his or her
"spouse" at the opening of the sandy cave which they

share. They peck at each other as if kissing. They usually mate for life, and they take equal responsibility for nurturing their young.

After the initial greeting, both of the mated penguins may move down their path, as if to "greet" their nearest neighbors with a friendly hello. Tiny clusters of four, six, or eight penguins can be seen "chattering" for ten minutes or longer. Before dark, all the penguins have made their way into the safety of their rooks, where they feed their young and spend a quiet night.

The next day, the mate that has returned stays behind to guard the rook while the other mate goes to sea. Like clockwork, the penguins again march to the water, hurl themselves through the crashing waves, and regroup beyond the surf line to form raftlike structures that will "float" the seas in search of food.

What a beautiful image of God's family these creatures provide for us, as they cheerfully live and work together in unity.

Stubborn as an Old Goat?

Even so now yield your members servants to
righteousness unto holiness.
Romans 6:19

*M*artin Luther had a favorite illustration he used in his sermons:

"*If* two goats meet each other in a narrow path above a *piece of water, what do they do?" asked Luther. "They cannot turn back, and they cannot pass each other; and there is not an inch of spare room. If they were to butt each other, both would fall into the water below and be drowned. What will they do, do you suppose?"*

As it happens, one goat will inevitably lie down while the other goat passes over him. Once the walking goat is safely on his way, the other will rise and continue on his chosen path. This way, both get where they wish to go safely.

There is a great deal of concern in today's world about allowing others to "walk all over us." But lying down to give way to another in order that both might achieve their goal is not the same as being a doormat. Nothing Jesus ever did could be considered weak and helpless. In strength and power He laid down His life for us. His example teaches us we must be willing to prostrate ourselves for others to follow His example.

Next time you come to an impasse with someone, consider what might happen if you simply yielded your pride for a moment and allowed the other person to

- speak his opinion,
- present his argument,
- offer his idea,
- suggest a course of action, or
- perhaps even make a decision.

Ask yourself, "Would this change the direction I am going in my life? Will it keep anyone from heaven?"

Prostrating ourselves for the benefit of others rarely costs us anything, but it may yield great rewards, both now and for eternity!

It Is Well

You will be like a well-watered garden,
like a spring whose waters never fail.
Isaiah 58:11 (NIV)

The creators of two popular comic strips each took a year off from work because they found it harder and harder to come up with fresh ideas.

The writer of a popular female-detective series of books took two years to finish her last novel instead of the usual one year, because she was having difficulty with the plot, and she wanted to get it right.

The star of a popular TV series asked to be let out of his contract after one season, because the demands of the show meant there was less time to be with his family.

When the well is running dry, you sometimes have to stop and let it rest.

Some people are gifted enough (or stubborn enough) to push themselves to their creative limits for weeks, months, or years on end. Some of them burn out at an early age or even die early from single-minded devotion to their work. Others, however, seem to go on forever.

How do those who continue do it? By pulling back now and then...by always keeping something in reserve...by knowing when to slow down or stop, if only for a brief time. They know the importance of keeping water in the well.

In our work, we sometimes "dry up" creatively. We assume our own wells of inspiration will always be full, so we don't bother to take opportunities to read, travel, attend performances, visit galleries, explore new places, or do other things that feed our creativity. We each need to take enough breaks from our work to receive input from others, especially those who have valuable lessons or skills to teach us.

Instead of sending our buckets down into the same well over and over again, let's leave them above ground now and then, and allow our wells to be refilled.

Taste Berries

Oh, that men would give thanks to the Lord
for His goodness, and for His wonderful works
to the children of men!
Psalm 107:8 (NKJV)

In Africa there is a fruit called the "taste berry," so-named because it makes everything eaten after it taste sweet and pleasant. Sour fruit, even if eaten several hours after the "taste berry," seems sweet and delicious.

For Christians, gratitude is the "taste berry" that makes everything else taste sweet. When our hearts are filled with gratitude, nothing that comes our way seems unpleasant to us.

Most often we are grateful only when we are happy with our circumstances or enjoy what we have been given. However, we may need to be taught like children to say "thank you" for what is given to us, whether we like it or not.

A habit of giving thanks in all circumstances helps us to look beyond our immediate situation and see our lives from a higher perspective.

Sometimes the gifts given to us may not appear to be good gifts or gifts we desire. But when we learn to thank God in all things, we discover that the gifts we've received are exactly what we need.

Gratitude can also help a person who is mourning, or lighten the load of a person carrying a heavy burden. It can dispel loneliness and give strength to a person in ill health.

George Herbert wrote this beautiful "thank-you" prayer:

Thou hast given so much to me,
Give one thing more — a grateful heart.
Not thankful when it pleases me,
As if Thy blessings had spare days,
But such a heart, whose pulse may be Thy praise.

Keep the "taste berry" of gratitude in your hearts and all of life will be sweeter.

Courage for Closure

Be strong and of a good courage; be not afraid,
neither be thou dismayed: for the Lord thy God
is with thee whithersoever thou goest.

Joshua 1:9

*A*lthough we generally associate courage with starting something, there is a certain type of courage required to bring a task to its proper conclusion. Why? Because the end of a project, tenure of time, or association signals:

• *Evaluation.* After the curtain comes down, will the audience applaud or shout with displeasure? Will our efforts be appreciated and rewarded or ridiculed and rejected? Many people find it easier to stall on the completion of a task than to bring things to a close. They fear criticism.

• *Change.* After closure, things change. Teams are dismantled and new ones formed. Routines may be altered. New responsibilities, duties, or tasks may be required. For many people, change is threatening. It requires effort, adjustment, and adaptation. People fear they may not be able to cope with or "fit into" a new scheme.

One of the most eloquent statements about courage was made by Martin Luther King, Jr., who said: "Courage is an inner resolution to go forward in spite of obstacles and frightening situations.... Courageous men never lose the zest for living even though their life situation is zestless; cowardly men, overwhelmed by the uncertainties of life, lose the will to live. We must constantly build dikes of courage to hold back the flood of fear."[34]

A "dike of courage" is forged within us when we accept the reality that the Lord governs every change in life. Nothing happens without His notice. He is Lord of all — beginnings, middles, and endings.

Furthermore, as we walk with Him we draw from His strength and power just as a branch draws sap from the trunk of a vine. (See John 15:5.) The courage Jesus had in facing the cross becomes our courage in taking up our crosses — obligations, duties, and responsibilities — on a daily basis.

Trust the Lord today to give you courage to close out the day and face a new tomorrow.

Fire!

Be pleased, O Lord, to deliver me:
O Lord, make haste to help me.
Psalm 40:13

It's usually about tea time when we realize that the clock's been moving faster than we have. So we break into a mental sprint to see if we can beat the clock to the day's finish line.

It's usually about this time of day when everyone and everything needs immediate attention. Sometimes we end the day thinking all we did for the last few hours was "put out brush fires." Consequently, the primary objectives of the day stand waiting for attention.

With the usual candor of children, one kindergartner shed some light on this late-afternoon dilemma. He was on a class field trip to the fire station to take a tour and learn about fire safety.

The fireman explained what to do in case of a fire. "First, go to the door and feel it to see if it's hot. Then, if you smell or see smoke coming in around the door, fall to your knees. Does anyone know why you ought to fall to your knees?"

The little boy piped up and said, "Sure! To start praying to ask God to get us out of this mess!"

What a good idea for those brush fires that break out in the heat the day! If we mentally and spiritually fall to our knees, we move our thoughts to God's presence around us and His authority over the circumstances we are facing.

Falling to our knees puts us beneath the "smoke" of confusion and enables us to breathe in gulps of reason, calm, and clarity. We are in a better position to see a way out of the burning room and move in an efficient and productive direction.

By giving us knees on which to fall, God has already answered our prayer for help. Bowing down for prayer reminds us Who has ultimate control over the situation and puts us in communication with Him. He allows us to see how to rescue the day from the afternoon crunch.

Sometimes your tea time becomes a "falling on your knees" time!

Not Perfect Yet

Accept one another, then, just as Christ
accepted you, in order to bring praise to God.
Romans 15:7 (NIV)

A teacher from New England lost his father during a surgical procedure. It was a death that should never have happened. Blood vessels ruptured unexpectedly and too large a dose of blood thinner caused massive, unstoppable bleeding.

The family had questions. What went wrong? Who erred? Was this cause for a lawsuit?

The teacher was chosen by other family members to confront the doctors and get to the bottom of things. Someone needed to answer for this, but his conversation with the doctors didn't go as expected.

The attending physicians were serious, cooperative, and professional in their demeanor. But when they were discussing the unforeseen problem with the blood thinner, something happened that changed the tone of the meeting. The teacher saw one of the doctors swallow — hard.

It was a simple thing, really, but it spoke volumes to the teacher. It reminded him he was talking to a human being, someone who had worked and trained for years to reach the peak of his professional skill...but all in all, he was still just a man. He wasn't perfect.[35]

Much as we like to put doctors on pedestals and treat them as if they should be all-knowing and error-free...doctors *don't* have all the answers. Only God can make that claim.

As the apostle Paul said, "How great are his wisdom and knowledge and riches! How impossible it is for us to understand his decisions and his methods!" (Romans 11:33 TLB).

We need to realize only God is God, and only He can be everything to us. No human being can ever fill His shoes. When we realize this, we can have compassion for one another as flawed but ever-learning people. Then we trust God to work everything out for our good, as He promises in His Word. (See Romans 8:28.)

The Person in the Mirror

Looking unto Jesus the author and finisher of our faith;
who for the joy that was set before him endured the cross,
despising the shame, and is set down at the
right hand of the throne of God.
Hebrews 12:2

$\mathcal{G}$ood manners grow naturally in people who are trying to follow Jesus' example. As His nature grows within us, the selfish nature with which we were born begins to recede into the background. Our attitudes toward others change along with our behavior.

Good manners are one result of allowing Jesus to live through us. They are simply an expression of selfless concern for others.

"Some of us are so full of ourselves," one writer has noted, "that we cannot see Christ in all His beauty.

"Some years ago, when I was away on a preaching appointment, my wife and little daughter stayed at the home of a friend. On the bedroom wall just over the head of the bed in which they slept there was a picture of the Lord Jesus, which was reflected in the large mirror of the dressing table standing in the bay of the bedroom window.

"When my little daughter woke on her first morning there, she saw the picture reflected in the mirror and exclaimed, 'Oh, Mummy, I can see Jesus through the mirror!' Then she quickly kneeled up to take a better look, but in doing so brought her own body between the picture and the mirror, so that instead of seeing the picture of Jesus reflected, she now saw herself.

"So she lay down again, and again she saw the picture of Jesus. She was up and down several times after that with her eyes fixed on the mirror.

"Finally, she said, 'Mummy, when I can't see myself, I can see Jesus; but every time I see myself, I don't see Him.'"

When self fills our vision, we do not see Jesus. This afternoon, when the events of the day and your personal concerns are heavy on your mind, turn your eyes to Jesus. Then see if you don't feel transported from the cross you have been bearing to His throne in heaven!

References

Unless otherwise indicated, all Scripture are taken from the *King James Version* of the Bible.

Scripture quotations marked NIV are taken from the *Holy Bible, New International Version®* NIV®. Copyright © 1973, 1978, 1984 by International Bible Society. Used by permission of Zondervan Publishing House. All rights reserved.

Scripture quotations marked NKJV are taken from *The New King James Version* of the Bible. Copyright © 1979, 1980, 1982, 1994 by Thomas Nelson, Inc., Publishers. Used by permission.

Scripture quotations marked NASB are taken from the *New American Standard Bible*. Copyright © 1960, 1962, 1963, 1968, 1971, 1972, 1975, 1977 by The Lockman Foundation. Used by permission.

Scripture quotations marked NRSV are taken from *The New Revised Standard Bible*, copyright © 1989 by the Division of Christian Education of the churches of Christ in the United States of America and is used by permission.

Verses marked TLB are taken from *The Living Bible,* copyright © 1971. Used by permission of Tyndale

Endnotes

1 *Teatime Collections*, Patricia Gentry (San Ramon CA: Chevron Chemical Co., 1988), p. 5.

2 *Daily Readings from the Works of Leslie D. Weatherhead*, Frank Cumbers, ed. (Nashville: Abingdon Press, 1968), p. 312.

3 *The Forbes Scrapbook of Thoughts on the Business of Life* (Chicago: Triumph Books, 1992), p. 111.

4 *Guideposts,* March 1996, pp. 10-13.

5 *People*, March 18, 1996, p. 62 .

6 *Ordering Your Private World*, Gordon MacDonald, (Nashville, Thomas Nelson Pub., 1984, 1985), pp. 152-153.

7 *Illustrations Unlimited*, James S. Hewett (Wheaton, IL: Tyndale House, 1988), pp. 410-411.

8 *Forgive and Forget: Healing the Hurts We Don't Deserve*, Lewis Smedes (NY: Harper & Row, 1984), pp. 86-89.

9 *Decision*, October 1995, p. 42.

10 *The Weight of Glory*, C. S. Lewis (NY: Macmillan, 1949), pp. 18-19.

11 *San Luis Obispo Telegram/Tribune*, March 9, 1996, p. C8.

12 *Reader's Digest*, April 1996, p. 116.

13 *San Luis ObispoTelegram/Tribune*, March 16, 1996, p. E4.

14 *The London Ritz Book of Afternoon Tea*, Helen Simpson (NY: Arbor House, 1986), p. 6-7.

15 *Encyclopedia of 7700 Illustrations*, Paul Lee Tan (Garland, TX: Bible Communications Inc., 1979), pp. 1477-1479.

16 *Teatime by The Tea Ambassador*, Aubrey Franklin (NY: Frederick Fell Publishers, Inc., 1981), pp. xi-xii.

17 *Psychology Today*, November/December 1994, p. 16.

18 *Daily Readings from the Works of Leslie D. Weatherhead*, Frank Cumbers, ed. (Nashville: Abingdon Press, 1968), p. 285.

[19]*Encyclopedia of 7700 Illustrations*, Paul Lee Tan (Garland, TX: Bible Communications Inc., 1979), p. 1477.

[20]*Ordering Your Private World*, Gordon MacDonald (Nashville: Oliver-Nelson, 1984, 1985), p. 177.

[21]*Teatime by the Tea Ambassador,* Aubrey Franklin (NY: Frederick Fell Publishers, Inc., 1981), p. 62.

[22]*Diamonds in the Dust*, Joni Eareckson Tada (Grand Rapids, Michigan: Zondervan, 1993), February 17 entry.

[23]*The Treasury of Inspirational Anecdotes, Quotations & Illustrations*, E. Paul Hovey (Grand Rapids, MI: Fleming H. Revell (Baker Books), 1994), pp. 204-205.

[24]Ibid., p. 223.

[25]*The Finishing Touch*, Charles Swindoll (Dallas: Word, 1994) p. 69.

[26]*Weavings,* January-February 1991, pp. 7-13.

[27]*Health*, March/April 1995, pp. 48-49.

[28]*Thesaurus of Anecdotes*, Edmund Fuller, ed. (NY: The Wise Book Co., 1945), p. 103.

[29]*Teatime by the Tea Ambassador*, Aubrey Franklin (NY: Frederick Fell Publishers, Inc., 1981), p. 4-5.

[30]*San Francisco Chronicle*, Feb. 4, 1996, p. 4.

[31]*Treasury of Christian Faith*, Stanley I. Stuber and Thomas Curtis Clark, ed. (NY: Association Press, 1949), p. 806.

[32]*Songs of My Soul*, W. Phillip Keller, compiled and edited by Al Bryant (Dallas: Word Publishing, 1989), pp. 100-101, 158.

[33]*Knight's Master Book of 4,000 Illustrations*, Walter B. Knight (Grand Rapids, MI: William B. Eerdmans Publishing Co., 1956), p. 261.

[34]*The Treasure Chest* (San Francisco: HarperCollins, 1995), p. 71.

[35]*Newsweek*, April 1, 1996, p. 21.

Additional copies of this book and other titles
in the *Quiet Moments with God* series and
God's Little Devotional Book series
are available at your local bookstore.

Breakfast with God
Coffee Break with God
Sunset with God

God's Little Devotional Book
God's Little Devotional Book for Dads
God's Little Devotional Book for Moms
God's Little Devotional Book for Men
God's Little Devotional Book Women
God's Little Devotional Book for Students
God's Little Devotional Book for Graduates
God's Little Devotional Book for Couples

Tulsa, Oklahoma